Bronzino, 1540–50, detail of *An Allegory with Venus and Cupid* (also called 'Venus, Cupid, Folly and Time'), oil on wood

Venus & Aphrodite

History of a Goddess

BETTANY HUGHES

First published in Great Britain in 2019
by Weidenfeld & Nicolson
This paperback edition published in 2020
by Weidenfeld & Nicolson
an imprint of The Orion Publishing Group Ltd
Carmelite House, 50 Victoria Embankment
London EC4Y 0DZ

An Hachette UK Company

1 3 5 7 9 10 8 6 4 2

A CIP catalogue record for this book is available
from the British Library.

ISBN (Mass Market Paperback) 978 1 4746 1038 4
ISBN (eBook) 978 1 4746 1039 1

Designed and typeset by Nici Holland
Printed in Great Britain by Clays Ltd, Elcograf, S.p.A

www.weidenfeldandnicolson.co.uk
www.orionbooks.co.uk

Contents

✳

Conclusion 205

Foreword

She spoke, and as she turned, her neck
Shone with roselight. An immortal fragrance
From her ambrosial locks perfumed the air,
Her robes flowed down to cover her feet,
And every step revealed her divinity.

. . .

And then she was gone, aloft to Paphos,
Happy to see her temple again, where Arabian
Incense curls up from one hundred altars
And fresh wreaths of flowers sweeten the air.*

---

* Virgil, *The Aeneid*, 1.494–514, trans. Lombardo

In the high-security storeroom in the heart of the ancient site of Pompeii a pair of beady, dark eyes stare out from the metal shelves. They belong to a foot-or-so-high limestone statuette of the goddess Venus.

The degree of survival is remarkable. Not only has Venus been left with full, glass-eyed sight (in spite of the massive volcanic eruption of Vesuvius in AD 79 which, at its most ferocious, threw 100,000 tonnes of magma per second into the air), but she is flushed with colour. Venus' hair is golden; her drapery, pink-blushed, tumbles off around her hips, skimming, but still revealing, her sex.

This is the Venus we think we know. Safe, attractive, chocolate-box-pretty. But the goddess of sexual love is in fact a far richer and more complicated creature than she at first appears. A potent idea, given a name and a face across five millennia, this deity is the incarnation of fear as well as love, of pain as well as pleasure, of the agony and ecstasy of desire. Venus is in fact the summation of the variegated, complicated business of human-heartedness – of our burning drive to engage with one another, both for good and for bad. She oversees the intensity of our passions and of our relationships within, and beyond, our species.

So, like the humans whose form she sometimes inhabited, the goddess of love has a richly complicated, tantalising, tricky, surprising and sensuous life story. For four decades I have followed the scent of her trail. It is a journey that has taken me to archaeological digs in the Middle East and archives in the chill of the Baltic; from the shores of the Caspian Sea to the nightclubs of Hoxton. Here is what I have found, an evolving history of the goddess of many kinds of love.

1

A Birth

Rising up from her mother the sea. Look,
The Cyprian, she whom Apelles laboured hard to
*   paint!*
How she takes hold of her tresses
Damp from the sea! How she wrings out the foam
From these wet locks of hers! Now Athene and Hera
Will say
In beauty we can never compete! *

---

* *The Greek Anthology, Planudean Anthology*, 16.178, second
century BC

Things do not start well.

Venus – or Aphrodite as she was originally called by the Greeks – was a primordial creature, said to have been born out of an endless black night before the beginning of the world.

Ancient Greek poets and myth-makers told this ghastly story of her origins. The earth goddess Gaia, sick of eternal, joyless copulating with her husband-son, the sky god Ouranos (sex which left Gaia permanently pregnant, their children trapped inside her), persuaded one of her other sons, Kronos, to take action. Gathering up a serrated flint sickle, Kronos frantically hacked off his father's erect, rutting penis and threw the

Aphrodite, assisted by two Horai – goddesses
representing the seasons – emerges from the sea on
the Ludovisi Throne. This relief was almost certainly
originally made *c.*480 BC for a temple in Locri, in
modern-day Calabria

dismembered phallus and testicles into the sea. As the bloody organs hit the water, a boiling foam started to seethe. And then something magical happened. From the frothing sea-spume rose 'an awful and lovely maiden', the goddess Aphrodite. This broiling, gory mass proceeded to travel the Mediterranean, from the island of Kythera to the port of Paphos in Cyprus.

But despite her violent and salty start, the young goddess, as she emerged from the sea on to the barren, dry land, witnessed a miracle: green shoots and flowers springing up beneath her feet. The radiant, enigmatic creature, followed by 'comely desire', was quite a sight to behold:

> *She set on her skin the garments which the*
> *Graces and the Seasons had made and dyed in*
> *the flowers of spring-time, garments such as the*
> *Seasons wear, dyed in crocus and hyacinth and in*
> *the blooming violet and in the fair flower of the*

rose, sweet and fragrant, and in ambrosial flowers

of the narcissus and lily. *

Aphrodite, an incarnation of fecund life, was accompanied, as she made her flower-sweet progress through the dusty earth, by gold-veiled Horai, the two Greek seasons of summer and winter, spirits of time and of good order. Born from abuse and suffering, this sublime force is being described to us not just as the goddess of mortal love, but as the deity of both the cycle of life and life itself. Aphrodite is far more than an attractive figure on a Valentine's Day card.

This is how many in Ancient Greece explained Aphrodite's birth. It is a story, with some variations (an alternate myth suggested that Aphrodite was the daughter of the king of the gods, Zeus, and the sea-nymph Dione), that was told and retold across the Mediterranean world. The ancients had a vivid mental

---

* *Kypria*, Fragment 4, transmitted in Athenaeus, 15.682D–E, trans. Breitenberger

picture of how their supernatural goddess of love and desire was conceived. Her psychological imprint was evident. But what about her physical trail? What does the archaeology in the ground reveal about the historical inception of Aphrodite and her adoration?

As we might expect, the material evidence offers a compelling alternative to the myth. Yet the truth of Aphrodite's origins is almost as strange as the fiction.

On the island of Cyprus there is a record of the celebration of the miracle of life, and of the sexual act, long before the Classical Greeks conceived of a voluptuous blonde they named Aphrodite. The life-giving powers of a spiritual, highly sexualised figure can be found in the formidable form of the so-called *Lady of Lemba*, a quite extraordinary limestone sculpture. Over 5,000 years old, this wonderful creature has fat, fructuous thighs, a pronounced vulva, the curve of breasts and a pregnant belly – and instead of a neck and head, a phallus, with eyes. The *Lady of Lemba* is in fact a wondrous mix of both female and male.

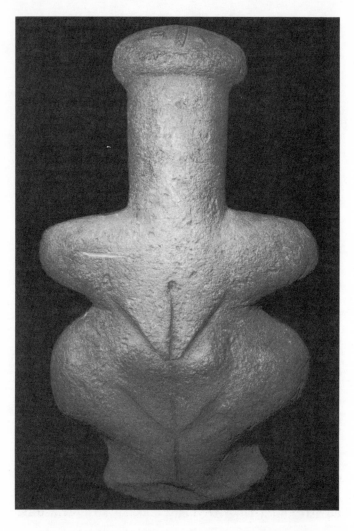

The *Lady of Lemba*, Cyprus, *c.*3000 BC, displaying both
a phallus / phallus neck and a vulva. Found at the site of
Lemba in 1976

I have had the privilege of studying this 'Lady' outside her glass case. Thirty centimetres tall, she pulses with power and potential. Discovered lying on her back, surrounded by other, smaller figurines, the *Lady of Lemba* is intriguing, a distant ancestor of our goddess of love. And she's not alone.

Probing deeper in time, back at least 6,000 years, we find the plateaux and foothills of western Cyprus were littered with tiny, pregnant stone-women, again with phallic-shaped necks and faces and pronounced female sex organs. These figurines – lovely things, crouching down, smooth to touch, an otherworldly soft green – were produced in huge numbers here. Many have pierced heads, so must have been worn as amulets. I first met these inter-sex marvels in the atmospheric back storerooms of the old Cyprus Museum in Nicosia. Lovingly laid in Edwardian wooden cabinets, they are an extraordinarily vivifying connection to a prehistoric past. A number of the figures, made of the soft stone picrolite, wear, as amulets, shrunken versions of themselves around their own stone necks. Dating from a time – the Copper Age – when the division of labour between women and men on Cyprus seems to have had parity, the majority of the enigmatic taliswomen-men were found in domestic spaces or near what could be prehistoric birthing centres. (Those mini-mes around their necks may represent unborn children.) Some of the basic stone-and-mud huts at one site, Lemba, have now been reconstructed. Shaded by olive trees, the prehistoric maternity wards make for a curious, sidebar of interest as tourists petrol-past on their annual sea-and-sand holidays.

Uberous, highly sexual figures, then, seem to have been central to social and ritual affairs on what came to be called, by the Athenian playwright Euripides in 405 BC, 'Aphrodite's Isle'. Along with these lubricious statuettes, sea-shells and a triton shell were also found, part of a ceremony whose form we can only imagine. Priestess-midwives wearing these potent insignia may well have aided births in the early Cypriot communities here, and these figurines probably protected homes and shrines; but there is no evidence yet of the full-blown worship of an identifiable goddess of sexual love.

So how did the goddess Aphrodite actually arrive on the island of Cyprus – Kypros in Greek? How was the deity, known variously in antiquity as Aphrodite, Venus and to many simply as Kypris, the Lady of Cyprus, culturally conceived and born?

Well, as ever, the myths get one thing right. Aphrodite did travel by sea.

2

Fornicating
& Fighting

Lady of blazing dominion
clad in dread
riding on fire-red power ...
flood-storm-hurricane adorned ...
battle planner
foe smasher ...

Inanna:
I will wrench your neck
grab your thick horns
throw you in the dust
stomp you with my hatred
grind my knees in your neck ...

fighting is her play
she never tires of it ...
a whirlwind warrior
bound on a twister ...
wild bull Queen
mistress of brawn
boldly strong ... *

---

* 'Inanna and Ebih', *c.*2350 BC by Enheduanna, the first-named female author in history, 1–44, trans. De Shong Meador. A prayer-poem describing the warrior aspects of the goddess Inanna, an ancestor in Aphrodite's family tree

Aphrodite-Venus is a complex creature – and in fact she has two births: on those shores of Cyprus as an early spirit of fertility and procreation, and as a ferocious warrior-goddess who is first made manifest east of Cyprus from Mesopotamia to Anatolia and across the Levant. Because in a region that spans modern-day Iraq, Syria, Jordan, Lebanon, Israel, Palestine, Turkey and Egypt, from at least 3000 BC onwards women and men watched one another, and generated in their minds a sex-and-violence deity to explain the tempestuous and desirous nature of human behaviour.

The bone evidence from this time tells us that this was an age of frequent antagonism and turbulence, an epoch of unbridled passions. In one burial mound at İkiztepe, Anatolia, dating from the Early Bronze Age, of 445 identifiable bodies, the young and the elderly alike have sustained serious head wounds and 43 per cent of men show signs of violent trauma. Most women of this epoch were mothers at twelve, grandmothers at twenty-four, dead by thirty. Men have axe cuts on their ribs and thighs, arrow shafts through their skulls, javelin strikes to their backs. Frequently we can tell that men, sometimes women too, were wounded in battle, patched up, and then sent back out to fight. And there seems to have been a sense that all lusts and urges – to make both love and war – came from the same place. Since this was a world where gods and demigods and spirits were believed to be everywhere and in everything, people conceived the notion that there were savagely lusty deities responsible for this messy volatility. They gave tumultuous desire a divine entity. No longer a mixture of male and female – fascinatingly, counter-intuitively

– as societies become more militarised and men edged into pole position, this ferocious creature was now all-woman. With premature death more likely, the earlier 'life-cycle' goddesses became predominantly harbingers of mortality. The wildness of war, and passion, took female form: across the Middle East, a kind of sisterhood of feisty warfare-and-wantonness goddesses – variously called Inanna, Ishtar and Astarte – started to emerge.

These goddesses were worshipped with particular fervency in the emerging cities of the age. In Babylon alone, Inanna presided over 180 sanctuaries. We hear from the *Epic of Gilgamesh* that the bustling, urban temples of Ishtar were places of worship, and also where goods and ideas were traded. When the Egyptian pharaoh Amenhotep III fell ill he requested that Inanna's statue be brought from her shrine at the metropolis Nineveh (modern-day Mosul) to him on the banks of the Nile in Luxor, hoping that the goddess's ferocious power might save his life. Frequently portrayed as young girls,

Burney relief, 'Queen of the Night' goddess with
tapering wings and talons, wearing a horned headdress
and elaborate jewellery. Nineteenth to
eighteenth century BC, made from fired clay
with red ochre pigment, currently in
the British Museum, found in Babylonia

'Horned Astarte', third to second century BC, made
from alabaster, currently in the Louvre, Paris, found in
the Necropolis of Hillah, near Babylon (*left*). 'Voluptuous
Ishtar', 1150–1110 BC, made from terracotta, currently
in the Louvre, Paris, found in Susa, from the Elamite
empire (*right*)

never settled, skittish, Inanna, Ishtar and Astarte were also the celestial beings originally associated with the planet we now call Venus. The brightest of all the stars, Venus' inconsistent peregrinations through the cosmos (at one point Venus was thought to be two separate Morning and Evening stars) signified in the minds of ancient communities these goddesses' vacillating nature, their need to travel and to conquer. The deities' power was thought to reside in the Venus-star itself. In 680 BC when the Neo-Assyrian king of Nineveh Esarhaddon summoned violators of a treaty to his court he thundered: 'May Venus, the brightest of the stars, before your eyes make your wives lie in the lap of your enemy …'

Ishtar was also honoured with the Ishtar Gate in Babylon, above which was emblazoned, 'she who vanquishes all'; Inanna, often dressed in refulgent white, was the fickle teenager of sovereign strength who never married but always broke hearts (as a bringer of war she sometimes appears with a beard);

and the divinity who could claim the closest genetic links to Aphrodite, often depicted on the prow of a handsome boat, was the Phoenician Astarte.

✳

If you travel from the rolling, red sands of Wadi Rum in the south of Jordan to the country's northern black-basalt deserts and through the fertile slopes above the Beqaa Valley in Lebanon, you will find surviving traces of the goddess Astarte, an early ancestor of Aphrodite-Venus. Like her Mesopotamian sister Inanna, whose hymn starts this chapter, Astarte, frequently portrayed with horns, was a creature who encapsulated war, death and destruction as well as the life-giving powers of sex. Astarte was worshipped across the region, her cult being particularly strong in the cities of Tyre, Sidon and Byblos. Aphrodite's classical sanctuaries were often built over Astarte's Bronze and Iron Age shrines.

One city sacred to Astarte was situated close to

modern-day Daraa in Syria, at Jordan's north border, mentioned in the books of Genesis and Joshua as Ashtaroth. When I was last there Assad's coalition bombs were pounding the region at night, destroying the shared heritage of East and West alike. During the day the sky was filled with Apache helicopters. The exquisite Roman theatre at Bosra was damaged by mortars; a number of fragments of statues of Aphrodite in Bosra's museum, some made of marble from the Greek island of Paros, are unaccounted for. Displaced Syrians were pouring across the border and lines of desperate refugees were waiting to be housed. Conflict felt very close. Experiencing this turmoil first-hand helped me to appreciate the dreaded power of Aphrodite's ancestors. This dynasty of goddesses were certainly not comfortable creatures. Desire – for control, blood, fear, dominance, rapture, justice, adrenalin, ecstasy – can lead both to making war and to making love, to churn and change of all kinds. Authors from Homer onwards have conflated the words used for military invasion and sexual penetration. In Homeric Greek, *meignumi* means both. *Eros* – love, passion and desire – was in the ancient world firmly paired with *Eris* – strife.

Through the widespread and fervent worship of goddesses of perturbing passions, we are starting to get a picture of ancient societies who recognised that desire can cause trouble. The ancestors of Aphrodite were the incarnation of that realisation. In the story of human society, the aboriginal Aphrodite was indeed lovely, but she was awful too, a creature of both day and night. Aphrodite and Venus were scions of an intimidating family tree.

Inanna, Ishtar and Astarte were also goddesses on the move. We can track the Eastern love-and-hate deities' journeys west where the goddess-head will soon be reconfigured and will eventually be given the name Aphrodite. To witness this fission and fusion we must leave the deserts of the Middle East and the mountainous drama of the Levant, and follow

Aphrodite's trail back to the legend-rich island of Cyprus.

✳

Make your way to the south-eastern shores of Cyprus, close to Larnaca airport, ignore the planes – and in the winter months, draw your eyes from the flocks of flamingos that land here on the salt marshes, visitors for 5,000 years – and you might just be able to make out archaeologists working on the dig of an ancient metropolis at Hala Sultan Tekke. To date, this is the largest Bronze Age city ever discovered: it spans up to fifty hectares, more than fifty football pitches.

The very presence of this wind-buffeted settlement tells of the humming interchange between traders and settlers on this island at the edge of Asia, Europe and Africa. The Eastern immigrants to Hala Sultan Tekke were people who brought with them strange new rituals, bull-worship and bull-slaughter, which they then appear to have melded with local fertility cults.

Along with the remnants of a city and its dead, among interloper archaeological riches being excavated each season originating from Ancient Egypt and Western Greece in the dun-brown mud, a glittering golden lozenge featuring the goddess Astarte-Ishtar has been discovered. The bellicose great-grandmother of Aphrodite was demonstrably making her way towards Europe. But, as we know, Astarte-Ishtar did not arrive in virgin territory.

After the age of those strange, strangely beautiful penis-headed figures, Cyprus started to revere a local priestess-goddess and High Queen – the *wanassa*. She seems to have been a kind of sensuous, cosmic majesty of nature, a queen who loved her perfumes. Recently excavated Cypriot perfume workshops from this period, dating back to 2000 BC, buttress the literary texts that tell us that a nature goddess was worshipped on Aphrodite's Isle with lustrous, perfumed oils.

Perfume was a boom export for the island, perfectly placed as it was to receive raw materials from three continents and boasting its own unique flora and fauna in a micro-tropical environment. Aphrodite herself was never anything other than odiferous: she was said to be washed by the Graces, and was recalled by Homer in *The Odyssey*, as bathing at Paphos in perfumed baths:

> *And Aphrodite, who loves laughter and smiles,*
> *[Went] to Paphos on Cyprus, and her precinct there*
> *With its smoking altar. Here the Graces*
> *Bathed her and rubbed her with the ambrosial oil*
> *That glistens on the skin of the immortal gods.*
> *And then they dressed her in beautiful clothes,*
> *A wonder to see.* *

So the Eastern goddess-queen Astarte-Ishtar took on the form of the Kyprian nature and fertility goddess,

---

* *The Odyssey*, 8.389–95, trans. Lombardo

The *kourotrophos* goddess-spirit of Bronze Age Cyprus, with a bird face, frequently shown nursing a young child in her arms. 1450–1200 BC, made from terracotta, currently in the Metropolitan Museum of Art (MET), from Nicosia-Ayia Paraskevi

and vice versa. Aphrodite was shape-shifting. Driven by what it was women and men on the ground wanted to believe about the story of their fast-developing world and their place within it, the mating of deities was generating a divine love-child.

This hybrid Cypriot goddess was sensuous in many ways. The goddess figurines we find on the island from this time are curious creatures with bird-like heads and double-pierced ears, often carrying babes in their arms. They seem to straddle both the mortal and immortal worlds, the natural and the supernatural. Frequently richly decorated with golden necklaces and hanging hoop earrings, the sublime beings – found right across the island – reminded locals and visitors alike that the Kyprian domain was a land of possibilities, an intercontinental crucible of civilisation. A good territory – for men and gods alike – to which to lay claim.

Cyprus was, at this time, increasingly, a cultural dynamo thanks to the island's luscious natural resources – in particular, its uniquely rich seams of copper. Today, as you drive through the landscape, you can still find scars of modern copper-mining close to prehistoric mineshafts. Sanctuaries of a female deity have been discovered next to many of the key copper-producing areas. Copper, as a vital ingredient of the commodity of the age, bronze, really mattered. We have brilliantly personal letters, the Amarna Tablets, discovered by the fertile, busy banks of the Nile in Upper Egypt and dating to around 1350 BC, written in the Middle Eastern lingua franca, Akkadian, describing the import of copper from Cyprus. Combined with tin, copper becomes bronze, the symbol and signifier of the Bronze Age world. Bronze can make light, lethal weapons. Communities craved it – and those who produced, traded and employed the new technology became rich warrior-heroes. Aphrodite's island, Kypros – 'Copper Land' – provided the dynamos for a rapidly changing human society, and the supernatural spirits who controlled these resources were thought to be bounty incarnate.

Wonderful jewellery was produced on the island at this time. Delicate bronze brooches. Golden diadems. Light-catching necklaces with fat cornelian beads. All inessential, essential commodities that fanned a new kind of materialism. There is even a solid-gold pendant in the shape of a pomegranate, the granular beads on its surface, carefully arranged in tiny triangles, giving this exquisite item a temptingly organic and strikingly modern feel. We should imagine Aphrodite's early spirit being honoured among the smoke and smuts and hiss and heat of the alchemy of bronze and gold production. Right through antiquity, fire and metallurgy were consistently central to Aphrodite's cult, almost certainly as a throwback to her prehistoric incarnation. Perhaps this is why, in Greek tradition, Aphrodite was said to have married the calloused forge god Hephaestus. She was brazen in a number of ways.

So, as well as being patrons of fornicating and fighting, Aphrodite and her ancestors were key spiritual players in a febrile cultural climate, a fluctuating world that was brutal and brilliant in equal measure. This goddess was a companion of civilisation and a summation of the ambitions of human society, both benign and malign: a multi-faceted, resplendent, frightful force. We hear from an Early Bronze Age poem-prayer for Inanna:

He gave me the high priesthood ...

[And then the list goes on:]

He gave me godship ... shepherd-ship ...
descent into the underworld ... ascent from the
underworld ... the dagger and sword ... the
black garment ... the colourful garment ... the
loosening of the hair ... the binding of the hair
... the standard ... the quiver ... the art of love-
making ... the kissing of the phallus ... the art of
prostitution ... the art of forthright speech ... the
art of slanderous speech ... the art of adorning

speech ... the cult prostitute ... the holy tavern

... the holy priestess of Heaven ... the art of song

... the art of the hero ... the art of power ... the

art of treachery ... the art of straightforwardness

... plundering cities ... setting up the

lamentations ... rejoicing of the heart ... deceit

... rebellious land ... the art of kindness ... travel

... the secure dwelling place ... the feeding-pen

... the sheepfold ... fear ... consternation ...

dismay ... the bitter-toothed lion ... kindling of

fire ... the putting out of fire ... the assembled

family ... procreation ... the kindling of strife ...

counselling ... heart-soothing ...*

Aphrodite in her earliest iterations was nothing less than a patron of the ferment and fulcra of the progress of culture. The 'Aphrodite principle' was pervasive. It was a passion to engage, to saturate life with experience

---

* Prayer-poem of Inanna, *c.*2500 BC, trans. Wolkstein and Kramer

and then to enjoy kicking back from the adrenalin rush of living life to its fullest extent. Born in the minds of motivated women and men, as a sponsor of desire and its satisfaction, the goddess would soon become a patron of extreme pleasure-seekers too.

Babylonian cylinder seal, c.1800–1600 BC, 1¼ inches (just over 3 centimetres) tall, currently in a private collection, UK. At this time Inanna was known as 'Lady of the Morning and Evening Star'

3

Party Queen

Celestial Aphrodite, Paphian queen, dark-lash'd
Goddess, of a lovely mien.[*]

---

[*] 'Orphic Hymn 56' to Chthonian Hermes, trans. Taylor
[adapted]

The early, Cypriot Aphrodite also incarnated humanity's love of gratification. The goddess comes fully into focus in a heady age. Around 1150 BC those beautiful Bronze Age civilisations were starting to collapse. A domino line of great cities fell, from Troy in the eastern Hittite empire to Mycenae, Tiryns and Thebes in the west – the latter settlements of the Mycenaean Greeks. The cause of this tumult is still hotly debated, the attacks of 'sea-peoples' in their cedar-wood boats from the Levant being the most persistent explanation. But recent core analysis from the bed of the Sea of Galilee confirms that the period 1300–1150 BC suffered devastating mega-drought. This climate catastrophe, combined with an acceleration in maritime technology, appears to have given those with piratical skills the upper hand. With the subsequent collapse of Mycenaean culture, migrants from Crete and mainland Europe started to nudge their way east and north across the Aegean Sea, bringing their own ideas of a goddess who, as Homer would put it, hid the secret of love beneath her girdle.

We are about to witness the birth of Aphrodite as we know her.

The marked evolution at this time of the figurines and sanctuaries on Cyprus tells us that now a same-sex, three-way dynastic marriage was taking place – between a Greek goddess of fertility and human relationships, herself influenced by contacts with the East, a Cypriot nature deity and the Eastern goddesses of sex and war.

Cyprus was one of the first, and most critical, ports of call for Early Greek travellers. When Western and Eastern culture collided in the south of the island, a remarkable sacred city was raised – Palaeo Paphos, (Old Paphos) which today overlooks the Eastern Mediterranean and whose peace is punctured by military aircraft from Paphos airbase a few kilometres away. Palaeo Paphos developed into the goddess's premier sanctuary, truly a world-beater.

For millennia this remarkable, vigorous, wind-buffeted spiritual centre was considered as paramount as Delphi in Greece, the 'navel of the earth'. Homer is the first to mention Paphos in literature and its 'smoking altar, perfumed with incense'. Unlike those of other deities, Aphrodite's altars were not polluted with animal sacrifice – despite her belligerent origins, the goddess of love seems to have lost her taste for blood – although she always maintains a decidedly Eastern delight in the burning of perfumed oils and incense. Indeed, right down to the early modern period, perfume bottles in the shape of the goddess were produced, a reminder of her ability to stimulate many senses.

Old Paphos was a heady place. Although systematically stripped of its luscious antiquities from the late Renaissance onwards, ongoing excavations are revealing what a truly remarkable site this would have been. It takes a good few hours to criss-cross on foot, and in its heyday would have been a riot of colour and sounds: cosmopolitan, buzzy, adrenalin-filled. There are clay models from Cyprus that show Bronze Age rites in full swing. People sit intently on stools and chairs. One poor would-be attendee appears to have been shut out of the sacred gathering and peers in through a window. On Cyprus you were either in on the ritual action or an outcast.

We are told, in the *Homeric Hymn to Aphrodite*, that the Paphos sanctuary was protected by Golden Gates, almost certainly made of bronze. There were rose gardens, sweet myrtle trees and lotus ponds. Roses, violets, lilies, poppies and lotus flowers were frequently woven into garlands for use in Aphrodite's cult. Apples, quinces and pomegranates (a fruit associated with sex and the blood of both life and death) were also sacred to the goddess. On one local, generously proportioned vase, a wonderful painting shows a goddess figure (or is it one of Aphrodite's priestesses? It is hard to tell ...) lounging and poised to suck alcohol, almost certainly mixed with opiates, through a straw. Opium-burners are found elsewhere on the island in the goddess's shrines. Framed by dancers and the tree of life, the sublime central figure appears to be wearing black-silk stockings. The scene is intense, animated, sprightly and sensual. Close by, a sphinx – half woman, half camel – sniffs a lotus flower, a natural aphrodisiac.

I have had the privilege of burying my nose deep into the centre of a freshly cut blue lotus flower, with its sun-gold stamens, taken from the waters of the Nile. The ancients believed this bloom was sacred because of its powers to transport those who used it. Blue lotus was added to wine, it was inhaled, turned into an oil, burnt in temples. Recent research has shown that the blue lotus does indeed have mild aphrodisiac and psychotropic qualities. It is a feel-good gift of the natural world.

So, we can hold in our mind's eye images of the vital popularity of the burgeoning Aphrodite cult. The goddess's many worshippers have been immortalised in the Cyprus Museum in Nicosia; wonderful little handmade clay figurines, some still with traces of their original paint, carrying flat baskets full of loaves of bread and cakes, garlands of flowers. The goddess at Paphos was offered honey, ointments, balms, foliage and fruits. There are even cake moulds in the shape of the divine women here with arms upstretched – a typical gesture of prayer, praise and of connection to the spirit realm. The goddess's cult was gingered up by music: tambourines, frame-drums, hand-drums, cymbals, the lyre. Four thousand fragmentary offerings to Aphrodite by pilgrims from Europe, Africa and Asia have been excavated at the Paphos sanctuary dating just from the years 1000–400 BC.

Even in the fourth century AD – at a time when Cyprus was nominally Christian – lamplights were being left to the female inhabiting spirit of the place, as they had been for centuries:

> *Meleager dedicates to you, dear Cypris, the lamp*
> *His play-fellow, that is initiated into the secrets*
> *of your night festival.**

But there is a mystery. The sensuous goddess of nature and love on Cyprus is often simply called The Queen or The Goddess. When and how did Aphrodite acquire her name? The authors of the Homeric poems, composing in the eighth and seventh centuries BC, describe the Paphian goddess as both Kypris and, what is to us the more familiar appellation, Aphrodite. Some Greeks claimed that 'Aphro-dite' meant foam-born (*aphros* in Greek is the word for sea-foam), but Aphrodite

---

* *The Greek Anthology*, 6.162, first century BC

is in fact much more likely to be a derivation of the Phoenician name Ashteroth (Hellenised as Astarte) – itself perhaps with Semitic roots that signify bright or shining. Our search for the origins of the moment when the goddess acquired the name Aphrodite is a challenge, hailing as she does from an era when prehistory and history grazed – when much of life remained textually unrecorded, and therefore has to be deduced from oral traditions and material remains.

But what is certain is that by the flowering of the Iron Age, in the eighth century BC, the goddess of desire had a new name, Aphrodite, and the sanctuary at Paphos was thought to be her most-favoured temporal home.

From this time onwards, the Paphian Aphrodite is depicted as a life-giving goddess with red breasts. Birds and doves hold special significance for her, as they did for one of her Middle Eastern ancestors; the Greek name for dove, *peristera*, almost certainly derives from the Semitic *perah Ishtar* – the bird of Ishtar.

Bronze doves, terracotta doves, marble doves, figurines holding doves as offerings have all been found at her shrines. At the Cypriot sanctuary at Idalion a dovecote has been lovingly teased out of red earth and left as a gift for the goddess. Aphrodite kept close hold of this billing and cooing bird – you can still find images of her with doves today, from the fine lines of François Boucher's erotica to less subtle erotic internet imagery.

Typically clothed, the Iron Age, animal- and bird-loving Aphrodite is always richly adorned, with roses and blossoms and finely wrought jewellery.

Because this goddess was so all-encompassing and belief in divinity so absolute, without her support women and men on the ground would have felt helpless. The evidence from graves of the time tells us this was an age of disease and stress: malaria, cancer and leprosy were all common. We should remember

François Boucher, *Venus Playing with Two Doves*,
c.1754, pastel on paper

that for these ancient communities the great goddess was not an optional extra, an idea that could be believed or dismissed: she was as real as the sky, as real as the sea. Without her, all was lost. Her presence gave hope. A massive Late Bronze Age wall still survives at Paphos. We can imagine Aphrodite's adorants taking shade here from that bright Mediterranean sun and those buffeting Near Eastern winds, as they fervently sought the power, the pity and the protection of the goddess. She was vividly imagined:

> *There she went in and put to the glittering doors,*
> *and there the Graces bathed her with heavenly*
> *oil, such as blooms upon the bodies of the*
> *eternal gods – oil divinely sweet, which she had*
> *by her, filled with fragrance. And laughter-loving*
> *Aphrodite put on all her rich clothes ... decked*
> *herself with gold ... For she was clad in a robe*
> *out-shining the brightness of fire, a splendid robe*
> *of gold, enriched with all manner of needlework,*

which shimmered like the moon over her tender

breasts, a marvel to see.[*]

That reference to 'laughter-loving' is important. It could simply mean joyful – and certainly, the goddess worshipped at Paphos on Cyprus has tenderised a little since her ancestors travelled from the mainland Middle East. But Aphrodite's laughter – and in particular her smile – is also a reference to a woman's sex. The worshippers of Aphrodite often employed shells in her cult, using them to decorate her shrines. This was possibly a nod to the goddess's oceanic birth – but there's more. Scallop shells were typically pierced so they could be worn around the neck in cultic ritual. The inside of a scallop shell looks remarkably, quite shockingly, like the female vulva and clitoris. The demotic Greek word *ketis* can mean both a scallop-like sea creature and a woman's labia and sex.

So the erotic temperature at Palaeo Paphos was set

---

[*] *Homeric Hymn to Aphrodite*, 5.58–87ff., trans. Evelyn-White

high. It is no surprise, perhaps, that according to legend, it was to Palaeo Paphos that Aphrodite travelled when she wanted to seduce the mortal Anchises, and where she fled, having been discovered in flagrante delicto, with her war-mongering lover-god Ares. The goddess was imagined at the Paphos sanctuary in many, heady ways.

But the brilliant thing about Aphrodite is that she is not just a creature of the imagination. Follow her material trail down time, and she acts as a barometer for the way the world has viewed desire and lust and the pleasures, purpose and preoccupations of flesh-and-blood women and men – and indeed of those who inhabited diverse points across the spectrum of sex and sexuality.

4

A Working Goddess & Working Girls

Aphrodite, you alone
Reign in power and honour,
Queen of all creation! *

Aphrodite Pontia, Aphrodite of the Deep Sea,
Aphrodite Limenia, Aphrodite of the Harbour†

your powers are subduing spells and charms which
bring all things mortal and immortal to your feet‡

---

* Euripides, *Hippolytus*, 1268ff, trans. Vellacott
† Pausanias, *Description of Greece*, 2.34.11
‡ Homer, *The Iliad*, 14.197

The first hard evidence of the name Aphrodite comes in fact not from Cyprus but from the lush little volcanic island of Ischia, in the Bay of Naples, where Elizabeth Taylor immortalised the power of sexual love during the making of the 1963 film *Cleopatra*.

Scratched from right to left on a simple terracotta cup, originally from Rhodes, dating to around 740 BC are the – tongue-in-cheek, given the charmingly humble nature of the pot – words:

> *I am Nestor's cup, good for drinking.*
> *Whoever drinks from this cup, immediately*
> *Desire will seize him for beautiful-crowned Aphrodite.*

Aphrodite first enters the written record, then, casually, mentioned by a carousing banqueter on an ancient wine cup as a patron of booze-fuelled sex. The goddess of love was frequently linked to Dionysos-Bacchus, the Greco-Roman god of ecstasy, transgression, transformation and excess, and to his gifts of wine. And although the mention of the Homeric king Nestor on the Ischian pot suggests an ironic connection to the high life, Aphrodite was a goddess dear to women and men of all degrees.

Once Aphrodite had a name – and so can be tracked in both written and archaeological records – it is apparent that she was multivalent and omnipresent, a goddess who was actively put to work in everyday lives in the service of many aspects of civilisation, from the mundane to the magisterial.

Aphrodite's story is central to the works of both Hesiod and Homer, in effect the 'bibles' of the Ancient Greek diaspora, so the goddess's name would have been on the tongues of many across the Eastern

Mediterranean from at least the eighth century BC onwards. She was also the eponymous heroine of the lost Greek epic the *Kypria*, attributed to Stasinus of Cyprus and composed as a prequel to *The Iliad*. Surviving only in fragment form, in the *Kypria* Aphrodite was styled as a key protagonist in the Troy story, tempting Helen to run away with Paris. Once again, we hear in this text that the goddess's redolent loveliness was admired:

> ... *in crocus and hyacinth and flourishing*
> *violet and the rose's lovely bloom, so sweet and*
> *delicious, and heavenly buds, the flowers of the*
> *narcissus and lily. In such perfumed garments is*
> *Aphrodite clothed at all seasons.*[*]

But – as her prehistoric origins suggest – this was more than just a love goddess. Aphrodite is, far more potently, the incarnation of MIXIS, a pervasive

---

[*] *Kypria*, Fragment 6, Athenaeus, 15.682 D, F trans. Evelyn-White

catalyst that was believed to mix things up; that encouraged (sometimes forced) intimacy, connection, collaboration. Aphrodite is the goddess with a close eye on the human species – those creatures who choose to live together in towns, villages, cities, states. It was she who was believed to encourage the carnal, cultural and emotional mingling of women and men; to inspire relationships across borders and boundaries. She made humans social beings and encouraged civic harmony. Her interests were Apollonian as well as Dionysiac. In fact, Aphrodite's power to unite, to nourish unity, was claimed by antiquity's authors from playwrights to philosophers to be the most potent in the universe, greater than that of the other gods.

✳

Because of her 'mix-it-all-up' nature and her marine birth, Aphrodite was also credited with protecting fleets that left dry land to sail out across open seas. Her sanctuaries are found particularly in port towns: think of Paphos on Cyprus, Corinth on the Greek mainland, Knidos in Asia Minor, Syracuse in Sicily, Piraeus near Athens and Pompeii on the Gulf of Naples.

Aphrodite-Venus in fact came to be Pompeii's premier deity – explaining the presence of that beautiful tinted statue that survives in the storerooms there. Pompeii's official title from 89 BC was *Colonia Cornelia Veneria Pompeianorum* – the Cornelian Colony of Pompeii under the Divine Protection of Venus. The city was dominated by a fine temple to the goddess, built in Carrara marble and accessed via a dedicated white marble-flecked road from the forum. Aphrodite-Venus' sanctuary guarded the harbour entrance to the town.

The goddess was a kind of mascot for Pompeii. She's often described in inscriptions in Pompeii as 'Venus Fiscia' – Venus who physics health, probably a reference to a pre-Roman health and fertility goddess who had originally been worshipped here on the fecund slopes of Vesuvius. If you are lucky enough to persuade one of Pompeii's guards to let you into the restricted Villa of Lucretius, you will find her delicately painted on the walls alongside her lover Mars. She can also be found in frescoes from the aptly named House of Venus and Mars, is depicted fishing in the House of Loreius Tiburtinus and in the storerooms of the Naples Museum, where an artist chose to portray the god of war cupping his lover's left breast.

One unfortunate woman from Pompeii's suburb of Oplontis died in the eruption wearing a golden armlet that shows Venus staring into a mirror held by Cupid, while back in Pompeii cheaper, bronze versions with a sea-wet Venus wringing out her hair survived the catastrophic eruption of AD 79. Lovers thanked her: 'If you don't believe in Venus, just look at my girl.' They also cursed her: 'I want to break Venus' ribs with sticks and smash her thighs. If she can pierce my tender heart why can't I smash her head?!' One wit scrawled

Roman fresco of the marriage of Mars and Venus, from
the *tablinum* in the House of Lucretius, Pompeii

a graffito next to an advertisement depicting Venus in a wool shop: 'What's the point of having a Venus if she's made of marble?' The goddess is even mentioned in the painted election posters that have survived: 'Vote for me, and the Venus of Pompeii will bring success to all you undertake!' In one Pompeian garden she appears again, in fresco form, floating languidly on a giant scallop shell, a companion for those frequent garden parties that took place in Pompeii – good wine to be drunk and food to be eaten, a sea breeze drifting in from the Mediterranean, mixing with the smell of bay and laurel and jasmine and rose that we know grew in the city.

Inevitably Venus is there too, to oversee some of the explicitly erotic scenes painted in workshops and homes and in the local brothel. When I was last in Pompeii, in a former baker's shop, investigating the remnants of lime-plaster still being mixed up on the very day of the disaster of AD 79, to patch up the mal-effects of the first phase of the geo-seismic activity during the

Vesuvian eruption, it was, frankly, a surprise to find highly erotic tableaux in the ante-chamber behind me. But then this was Venus' town, and Pompeii always feels like one of those sailor-ready, seaside party places where 'what happens abroad, stays abroad'.

And perhaps unsurprisingly, given her connection to both sea and sex, Aphrodite was the goddess not just of ports and port towns, but also of prostitutes. Indeed, we hear from both Roman and Greek sources that she was considered the patron saint of 'the oldest profession'. The Republican Ennius, a man of letters with a great interest in Greek works, and described as the father of Roman poetry, no less, asserted (in a translation of the Greek author Euhemerus) that Venus was originally a woman who actually invented prostitution, and whom then came to be worshipped as a goddess:

Venus was the first to establish the art of
prostitution and introduced it among women

*in Cyprus so they could derive profit from their
bodies by making them public property**

✳

Ennius wasn't entirely off the mark. In Classical
Greece, Aphrodite Pandemos, 'Common Aphrodite;
The People's Aphrodite', was hailed as the patron of
prostitutes and of rough sex. Aphrodite Pandemos was
worshipped before the entrance to the Parthenon in
Athens – her own temple, we are told by the North
African author Athenaeus, paid for by the proceeds of
the city's lucrative brothels.

A remarkable archaeological discovery in the
now pleasantly sylvan Athenian cemetery area of
Kerameikos, where, from the sixth century BC, foreign
sex-workers would wait for trade, shows how dear
she was to the poor girls, and young men, who lined

---

* Lactantius, *Divine Institutes* 1.17.9–10 = Euhemerus
Testimonium 75A Winiarczyk = *Brill's New Jacoby*, 63F25

up in the stalls, attending customers – what Athenians euphemistically called 'middle-of-the-day marriages'. As well as portable, rough figurines of both Astarte and Aphrodite that have recently been excavated, a remarkable hammered-silver medallion has been found here, probably some kind of a wall hanging. On this unique find, Aphrodite rides a goat through the night sky with Eros as her companion. Kid-goats and doves frolic across the scene, another young, naked boy leads the way in front of the goddess. A ladder – the Ancient Greek word for ladder is *klimax* – is propped up behind the determined-looking deity. (A common ancient phrase for climactic orgasm was 'Aphrodite's finishing post'.) The sexual metaphors abound. One can only hope the presence of the goddess in this liminal, pullulating, pulsating corner of the cosmopolitan city-state brought some comfort to the pitiful sex-slaves who lived here, weaving by day and being shagged by night – so cheaply, an *obol* a time, that even slaves could afford to buy their wares.

A marginally better place for the *pornai* to operate would perhaps have been a five-hour horse-ride south-west of Athens, at Corinth. The splendid Temple of Aphrodite here, reached by a sweaty climb of four kilometres up the unfeasibly high, mottled-grey rock, was said to be packed with prostitutes ready to serve maritime travellers who came from North Africa, and from Eastern islands such as Chios and Cyprus. The plethora of erotic scenes found on vases and metal-ware here – and now discreetly stored in a private back area of Corinth's museum – certainly suggest that the sanctuary under Aphrodite's purview saw a good deal of sexual activity, both homosexual and heterosexual.

So were the prostitutes and courtesans who operated out of Aphrodite's temples and precincts sacred? This is a gnarly issue. Ancient sources firmly tell us that there was sacred prostitution employed in honour of, and for the material benefit of, Aphrodite at her sanctuaries at Corinth, Paphos and elsewhere.

Mirror cover originally from Corinth, *c.*340–320 BC,
bronze and silver, 17½ cm diameter, with Eros and erotic
scene (*symplegma*), currently in the Museum of
Fine Arts, Boston

Herodotus, the Father of History, documents unequivocally that in the sanctuary of Mylitta – one Eastern name for Aphrodite in Babylon – women prostituted themselves for the goddess (however rich or poor, all women, Herodotus elaborates, were forced to do this once in a lifetime), and that there were similar practices in certain sanctuaries in Cyprus. The theme is eagerly taken up by many authors from antiquity: we hear of Aphrodite's sacred prostitutes in Lebanon, Syria-Palestine, Kalydon, Salamis, Eryx in Sicily . . . the list goes on. Aphrodite's sanctuaries on Cyprus were described by some as being thick with sacred sex-workers, and later Christian authors were ready to condemn this 'diabolic' practice. We hear that in the sanctuary of Amathus on Cyprus, 'there was a great crowd of pagans, indecent women and men fussing around them'.*

Certainly, there is evidence of intercourse in

---

* *Acta Barnabae*, 20–21

Achna bowl from 600–800 BC, made and found in Cyprus.
The bowl contains a complex frieze of figures, some
depicting sex scenes, arranged around a central rosette

connection with the divinity – an intriguing bowl from a tomb near Achna on Cyprus shows women sniffing lotus flowers and having enjoyable-looking sex in a sanctuary. And following the construction of the Equestrian Centre for Athens's 2004 Olympics, a complex sacred to Aphrodite – an Aphrodiseion – was discovered at the suburb of Merenda, the ancient deme of Myrrhinous. Here, a charming courtyard has been planted with trees. Accessed by a bathing area with plaster-lined baths, there are offerings of drinking vessels and beehives, and, tellingly, mention of a famous courtesan of the time, Nannia. But the wealth of imagination (all historical accounts of sacred prostitution that exist are written by men) about being able to pay for a sacred screw seems to be greater than the hard evidence available for the practice of common-place transactional sex in honour of the goddess.

Then common sense kicks in. At a time when sex and its transformational, transcendental, ecstatic qualities were codified but not considered sinful, and were often all that a woman (from the age of eleven or so, the sources tell us) had to sell, it would perhaps be stranger if both the buyer and the seller had not wrapped the chance for casual sex in a religious mantle. Boys too were at times put 'in service' of the goddess. So sacred prostitution would be odd, not if present, but if absent. It is a sobering thought that the greatest trade in prostitutes came from the human booty of warfare; prostitutes were truly Aphrodite's children, since she was a patron of both copulation and of conflict.

✳

Aphrodite, as well as sponsoring casual carnal encounters, was employed in ancient cultures as a profitable protector of marriage and conception.

Classical Athenians told one another that it was the great lawmaker himself, Solon, who had established the Temple of Aphrodite Pandemos on the city's famous

Acropolis rock. The message being transmitted was that even sexual urges were now in the purview of the state. Solon was said to have founded this temple with the proceeds of a brothel that he set up to harvest the appetites of the young men in the city. And come the fifth century BC, as Athens entered its 'Golden Age' and citizenship was restricted only to the children of citizens (no outsiders, no foreigners allowed), Aphrodite as marriage-maker (and maintainer) became evermore central to the city-state's political make-up. Recent re-evaluation of the evidence suggests that the democrat-reformer Cleisthenes may have had coins minted with Athens's patron goddess Athena on one side and Aphrodite Pandemos on the other. As life grew more demanding, more complex, Aphrodite was increasingly invoked and honoured to nourish the harmony and stability of the progressive Athenian polis.

When a new metro system was constructed in Athens before the 2004 Olympics, many pots showing Aphrodite at weddings emerged from the sticky earth. Down by Kerameikos station – then the wrong side of the tracks, now a hipster hangout – a charmingly decorated vase appeared, typical of fashions in the city. A bride-to-be sits neatly while one of Aphrodite's Erotes (the goddess's retinue of winged godlets) and Eros (her consort-son) fly in to bring the young girl good fortune. Every fourth day of the month was sacred to Aphrodite and she was worshipped in a popular pan-Hellenic festival, the Aphrodisia. In one version of the Aphrodisia in Thebes the lucky local general celebrated the end of his term in office by getting his secretary to source for him 'the most stately and beautiful women of Thebes to spend the night ... very pleasantly'.* There is, though, a rather dark conclusion to this tale: the courtesans sourced turned out to be a honey trap, assassins in disguise. As ever with the goddess, sex and death are close consorts.

---

* Xenophon, *Hellenica*, 5.4.4

Whether within or beyond the marriage bed, classical Aphrodite was believed to have a practical and political job to do. But she was not just a champion of what some judged to be orthodox sex and desire. She was also a champion of sexual fluidity and experimentation.

5

Ta Aphrodisia – The Things of Sex

You can turn man into woman,
Woman into man[*]

_____

* 'Lady of the Largest Heart', a hymn to Inanna by Enheduanna,
*c.*2300 BC, trans. adapted from De Shong Meador

Aphrodite was a torchbearer for explorations into sexuality as well as sex. At Amathus, one of her main sanctuaries on Cyprus, an intriguing figurine was discovered, buried in a tomb. This particular mini-sculpture shows the goddess with thick facial hair. The figurine has a splendid wig, a fine beard, and under her/his gauzy dress visible breasts and a vulva. Elsewhere in the sanctuary non-binary figurines have been found and in the sanctuary of Golgoi, also on Cyprus, a hermaphrodite priest holds a dove – Aphrodite's sacred bird. The Hellenistic historian Paeon of Amathus (as quoted by the lexicographer Hesychius) documented that Aphrodite could sometimes take the form of a man.

Priest of Aphrodite with breasts and votive dove,
limestone, sixth century BC from the sanctuary of Golgoi,
Cyprus. The priest's robe is decorated in a lotus motif

In two fragments (325a and b) from a long-lost play, the stellar Athenian playwright Aristophanes concurs, informing his audience that the cult of Aphrodite-Aphroditos – She-He Aphrodite – was introduced to Athens from Cyprus.

Now there are a number of things going on here. It could be that an Eastern practice, where the priests of Inanna, Ishtar and Astarte were sometimes androgynous or eunuchs or transgender/intersexual, is being remembered. Those sexually polyvalent figures could recall the Greek tradition of Aphrodite's salty birth: some believed that the young goddess kept her father's castrated male sex organs within her. The Amathus figurine and the hermaphrodite priests could be a figurative version of the abstract Lady of Lemba, or simply an early recognition of the non-binary nature of sex and desire.

Indeed the very term 'hermaphrodite' derives from the Greek legend that the union of Aphrodite and the god Hermes resulted in a beautiful child who was merged with a nymph to become a deity with both female and male sexual characteristics. During sacrifices to Hermaphroditos, also called Aphroditos, on Cyprus, male and female cult-followers exchanged clothes by moonlight. The god-goddess, as Aphroditos, was commemorated on Cyprus with a cult statue that enshrined the double-sex divinity.

✳

It is a homoerotic female author from antiquity who treats Aphrodite with most nuance and respect. Composing on the island of Lesbos, just off the coast of Asia Minor, in the seventh century BC the poet Sappho dedicates much time – and many lines – to immortalising her own intimate relationship with the goddess of love. Today Lesbos is still enchanting, the light seems to play here in a special way – and if you visit Sappho's birthplace near Mytilene you can identify the shivering oak leaves, the fragrant banks that the poetess describes in her lovely, lyrical works.

Sappho's 'Ode to Aphrodite' hymns a lambent temple to the goddess surrounded by apple trees, roses and spring flowers. Digs show that this is not a flight of poetic fancy, but a record of the reality of seventh- and sixth-century BC life. Definitely an aristocrat, probably a high priestess of Aphrodite, with well-born girls in her charge, Sappho's job seems to have been to teach young women how best to navigate life's pleasures and pitfalls. The remarkable Polyxena Sarcophagus, discovered in 1994 in the Granicus River Valley not far from Lesbos in what is now Anatolian Turkey (the Granicus springs in the foothills of Mount Ida, where a young Prince Paris was said to have made his Judgement, choosing Aphrodite as the fairest of all the goddesses), is an extraordinary survival from Sappho's age. As well as the blood sacrifice of Polyxena as her throat is slit, it shows women having animated conversations at a Sapphic Symposium. We can imagine Sappho in a similar situation with her precious, impressionable charges as she taught them of Aphrodite's art; of limb-loosening desire, of silvery moons, and fire creeping under your skin when you start to yearn for another:

Mother darling, I cannot weave –
slender Aphrodite – the Kyprian goddess – has
broken me with longing.[*]

Sappho's conversations with Aphrodite, which were so popular in antiquity that they have survived in quite some number, copied out on papyri and preserved in the desert sands of Egypt, are personal, conspiratorial. The goddess is Sappho's confidante. Together the two explore how best to express love, and the fact that love – as Sappho puts it for the first time in recorded history – is 'bitter-sweet' (although Sappho is a little more honest and says love is sweet and then bitter). Plato

----

[*] Sappho, Fragment 102

honoured Sappho, nominating her the Tenth Muse. The frequency of the discovery of new lines of Sapphic poetry on papyri fragments – even within mummy cartonnage, used to mummify humans, crocodiles, cats – is testimony to her widespread reach and use. In 2014 a new fragment of a Sappho poem, 'The Kypris Song', was identified from folded papyri cartonnage probably used to bind a book. The wonderful, imploring work describes the vertigo of loving and losing love:

> *How can someone not be hurt and hurt again,*
> *Queen Aphrodite, by the person one loves*
> *and not want above all less suffering?*
> *What do you have*
> *in mind, to idly rend me shaking*
> *from desire loosening knees?* *

Appealing directly to the goddess, Sappho reminds us, as Aphrodite reminds us, that intimacy and compassion

---

* Sappho, 'Kypris Song', Fragment, trans. Rayor

and companionship – as well as desire – are important constituents of love:

> *... you demanded what*
> *it was now, and why I called now, and what*
> *my maddened heart most*
> *wanted ...*

> *Please come to me: release me from driving*
> *care and all my heart longs*
> *to accomplish, accomplish.*
> *Be my ally.**

Aphrodite was a divine incarnation of the many possibilities of the world. She nourished sexuality of all forms as a surging life force. Her various guises seem to be an early admission that there are many ways to feel, and to love. But the goddess's sway over sex meant she was considered by many to have not just heavenly but also demonic powers.

---

* Sappho, 'Ode to Aphrodite', Fragment, trans. Carson

6

Manikos Eros

She is death and undecaying life,
she is the rage of madness[*]

... love is alert
In all seasons.
Love is a north wind
On fire with lightening-flashes
Sent by the Kyprian.
It brings withering madness
It is black, it is shameless,

Our hearts through and through
Are wrung by its violence.[†]

---

* Sophocles, Fragment Tragicorum Graecorum Fragmenta 41
† Ibykos, Fragment 6, sixth century BC, trans. Aharon Shabati

So, at what point does this sublime and all-pervading power – *ta aphrodisia*, sex, the things of Aphrodite – become problematic?

Because as well as being a potent force behind all lusts and urges, our Queen of Desire was given many, rather less-than-flattering epithets. She was Philommedes, lover of male genitals (thanks to her unorthodox birth). But she was also Epistrophia, the deceiver; Melanis, she of the dark night. She was Kataskopia, the spying one; Psithyristes, the whisperer; Heliokeblepharos, the coy eyelidded; Tumborukhos, gravedigger and Androphonos, killer of men. And, most popularly in the ancient world, Aphrodite came to be known as Mechanitis, the deviser, a creature who meddled in and directed human affairs.

You could argue that much of this was thanks to Homer, or at least to the Homeric tradition. It all began with the question of *casus belli*: who was responsible for the greatest and most devastating war in myth-history – the Trojan War, that legendary, epoch-forming event, which, as Hesiod put it, 'destroyed ... a god-like race of hero-men ... for rich-haired Helen's sake'.* Many argued that the root of all the trouble was not Helen or Paris, or their lust for one another, but the female force who brought strife to mankind – Aphrodite.

On Greek black-figure ware, Aphrodite, with sinister determination, pops Helen of Troy in her lap to explain her fate – to follow love and to bring untold suffering to untold men. An excess of love for the Trojan prince Paris will bring with it excessive killing. As the enactors of Aphrodite's will, these two teenagers,

---

* Hesiod, *Works and Days*, 11.156f

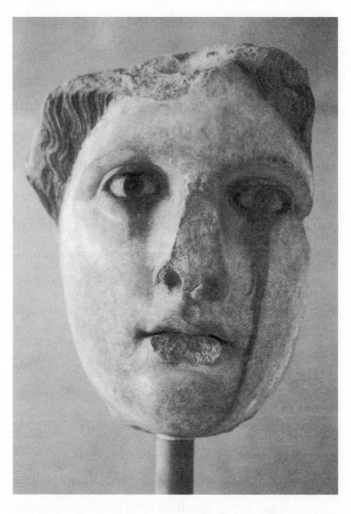

Goddess head, belonging to Aphrodite or Athena,
Acropolis Museum, Athens, third to first century BC.
A marble copy of a gold and ivory statue
from the Classical period

Helen of Sparta and Paris of Troy, do not have a chance. From the moment when Aphrodite prepared herself to meet Paris on Mount Ida before his Judgement, dressed finely in cloth perfumed with crocus and violet and rose, the course of fate was set. Little surprise that Aphrodite was sometimes equated with, and confused with, the goddess of fate and retribution, Nemesis.

This was truly, in the minds of the ancients, a love triangle. Where Helen of Troy went, Aphrodite followed. She is there on vases, welcoming Paris in, preventing Helen from escaping her inevitable adultery. She is there on the battlefields and in the royal bedchamber at Troy. She fires up the Spartan queen. Paris burns for his Greek paramour. The ancients knew only too well that although fire brought warmth and light to civilisations, it could also destroy. On tomb walls in Egypt humans have to pass through a torment of flames before they can become immortal. The archaeological record tells us that pyretic damage was one of the greatest disrupters of both town and rural life. Aphrodite is incandescence in goddess form.

The Roman poet Ovid picked his words with care when he describes how Paris, 'on fire with love', proclaims:

> One of our seers sang that Ilion would burn
> with the fires of Paris – that was the torch of my
> heart, as now has come to pass! ... Like a great
> queen you will make your progress through the
> Dardanian towns and the common crowd will
> think a new goddess come to earth; wherever
> you advance your steps, flames will consume the
> cinnamon ...!*

As late as the seventh century AD, the last of the Church Fathers, Isidore of Seville, catalogued in his *Etymologies* – a kind of encyclopaedia of all knowledge, a '*summa*' of the universe – the Trojan War as one of the 132

---

* *Heroides*, 16.123–5, trans. Showerman

critical events that had shaped the world.

And history's authors were quick to point out that Aphrodite-Venus did not work alone: her meddling son-consort Eros – like the goddess, thought to have been born out of a kind of primordial night – was her closest ally. Homer was the first to articulate Eros' sinister power: 'irresistible longing laid me low . . . I have never been in the grip of a desire so sweet', says Paris as he recalls his first night with Helen. Aphrodite's boy Eros drives men mad with his poisoned arrows. These weren't just literary flights of fancy, but strongly held beliefs. The philosopher Socrates describes the impact of love as equivalent to that of being bitten by a venomous spider or stung by a scorpion. And although it is a cupid, typically male, behind the bow-string, increasingly the debilitations of love were considered the fault of the mortal daughters of Aphrodite – of women. Not only was Aphrodite a home-breaker, but increasingly sex with all women was seen as a distraction from a truly fulfilling life, from male companionship and from the manly business of fighting and empire-building.

The evidence in the ground charts this gendered recast. As civilisations got greedy – ravening for more; more cities, more gold, more land – societies became ever more dependent on military muscle. It was impossible to invade another's territory without a reliable army. As geopolitics shifted, the female role in society – both mortal and divine – was increasingly marginalised. Women once kept society stable by birthing the next generation; now heroic men took on the role of society's saviours (the word 'hero' shares a root with *vir*, and literally means a saving male), strong-men heroes who could be relied upon to both defend and attack. Women, rather than being mankind's salvation, started to become creatures resented for merely sitting at home and bearing broods, sowing replacement spear-fodder. Instead of a true Pantheon of gods, a pecking order developed in the heavens with a single, smiting, male god at the top and in charge.

So, follow the trail of Aphrodite in literature and art through time and you chart the magnetic pull of a male-dominated society towards escalating misogyny. Attitudes to the goddess, in many quarters, reflected attitudes to flesh-and-blood women. And this sorry tale can also be told from evolving perceptions of the body of the goddess herself. A prurient fascination is spawned.

Although the goddess is described in archaic verse as having breasts 'shining like silver', what is being commemorated here is not her curves, but her riches. Golden Aphrodite is imagined thus: 'the gold-filleted Hours . . . clothed her with heavenly garments: on her head they put a fine, well-wrought crown of gold, and in her pierced ears they hung ornaments of orichalcum and precious gold, and adorned her with golden necklaces over her soft neck'.*

---

* *Homeric Hymns* 5.87–88 and 6.1–18, trans. Evelyn-White

Orichalcum was thought to be a mythical precious metal; it is mentioned, for example, in Plato's account of the legendary Atlantis. Until recently orichalcum was believed perhaps to be a description of platinum, but the discovery of thirty-nine ingots dating from the fifth century BC in a shipwreck at Gela, just off the coast of Sicily, indicates that in fact this was an interesting and rare metal alloy, a mixture of copper and zinc with small percentages of nickel, lead and iron. It is a metal fitting for this special goddess. As well as being adorned with peerless orichalcum, Aphrodite was also said to be clad in a mantle 'brighter than the flame of dawn'. She is dressed in 'fine garments', with 'twisted bracelets'. The goddess we imagine to be typically naked was, in fact, through much of antiquity, typically clothed.

But then she starts to shed her raiments.

From the fourth century BC onwards, Aphrodite is systematically stripped. The premier example, one of the most famous representations of the goddess of all time, is the so-called *Knidian Aphrodite*. Almost certainly sculpted by the master Athenian artist Praxiteles, this iconic artwork was the first full-size, fully naked stone sculpture of the female form in history. Although the original (after a brief sojourn in the city of Constantinople) has been lost, the *Knidian Aphrodite* inspired a myriad of copies. Always turning slightly away from the viewer in front of her, head delicately bowed, a sensuous hint of a smile on her lips, her hand fluttering to half-conceal her sex, this is a goddess who is coy about her lovely womanly body – arguably, even, ashamed of it. She obscures her sexuality while at the same time drawing attention to it. The original sculpture was commissioned for Aphrodite's Temple at the lucent maritime settlement of Knidos, just down the Anatolian coast from the location of the recently excavated Polyxena Sarcophagus.

The Knidians loved their nude version of the goddess; the nearby island of Kos, incidentally, also chose to order a life-size Aphrodite from Praxiteles,

The Ludovisi *Knidian Aphrodite*, second century AD.
A Roman marble copy of the orginal by Praxiteles
(*c.*350 BC), restored in the seventeenth century, currently
in the National Roman Museum, Rome

although Kos's version was clothed. The lightly painted and buffed, marble goddess of Knidos became a cause célèbre. A double-port in what is now south-western Turkey, Knidos was easy to access. Many pilgrims made the journey here to visit this controversial artwork. Rumours abounded that the sculpture was so achingly sexy because Praxiteles had used his own courtesan-partner Phryne, a famous Athenian beauty, as a model.

One anonymous author (whose work is preserved in Appendix 159 to the *Anthology of Planudes*, the thirteenth-century Byzantine magpie of ancient texts) mused: 'Who gave a soul to marble? Who saw Kypris on earth? Who wrought such love-longing in a stone? This must be the work of Praxiteles' hands, or else perhaps Olympus is now bereaved, since the Paphian has descended to Knidos.'

And again, from the Planudean Appendix 160, a passage once attributed to Plato, we hear:

*The Paphian-Kythereian Queen came through the
waves to
Knidos, wishing to see her own image, and having
Viewed it from all sides in its open shrine, she cried,
'Where did Praxiteles see me naked?'*

No one could deny the sculpture's charms. There is a horrible story told about Knidos's treasure. Because of a clever entrance design in the temple itself, the stone goddess was visible from both front and back. One young man was said to have been so enraptured with the goddess that he stole in at night and made love to her, ejaculating on the sculpture's thigh and permanently staining the Parian marble.

A trend had been fuelled. Aphrodite-Venus would find it very hard to keep her clothes on, and to command serious respect. Interest in Aphrodite-Venus gradually becomes excitement less about her potency than about her beguiling body.

From the second century BC onwards this realistic, Knidian nude variation on Aphrodite – a kind of virtual fantasy female – was hugely popular and copies were ordered again and again. In many reproductions Aphrodite-Venus seems increasingly ashamed of her nakedness, covering herself with myrtle (an evergreen plant with pungent white flowers, medicinal properties similar to aspirin and a mild aphrodisiac), a flower associated with the goddess since prehistory.

Versions of the *Knidian Aphrodite* were commissioned not just by men but by women too: the wives of the emperors Hadrian (Sabina), Marcus Aurelius (Faustina the Younger), Septimius Severus (Julia Domna), Caracalla (Plautina) and others – all effective and influential in their own right – wanting to associate themselves with the goddess's allure and dominion, had coins minted boasting a naked Venus in the Knidian form.

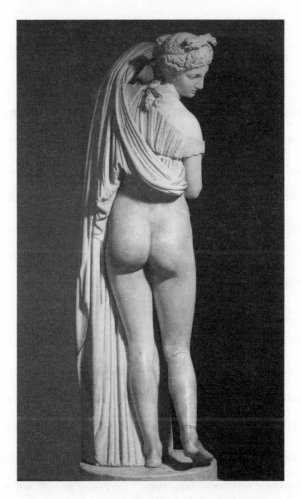

Venus Callipyge ('Venus with the beautiful buttocks'),
first or second century BC. A marble Roman copy of a
Greek original from *c.*300 BC, currently in the National
Archaelogical Museum, Naples, found in the area of the
Domus Aurea, Rome

✳

Another incarnation of the goddess, popular in antiquity, was far less coy. *Aphrodite Kallipygos* – Aphrodite of the Beautiful Buttocks – seems to have been actively adored in the ancient world. We hear that there was a cult of this beauty at Syracuse in Sicily. The story – first reported in the *Deipnosophists* (a fascinating volume, 'The Dinner-party Philosophers', written by that North African-based Greek author Athenaeus in the late second century AD) – went thus: following the example of two sisters who vied to have the best backside, young girls at beauty contests, judged by local farmers, were awarded best-buttock prizes. Although this feels like a bit of ancient smut, these beautiful-bottom contests are historically attested. Interestingly, recent work by the clinical anatomist David Bainbridge suggests that the higher reserves of lipids in the bodies of some females can result in increased levels of intelligence in both the women and their children. Maybe the Greeks were on to something. Fine-bottomed Aphrodite was a role model for an appealing psycho-physical package.

But as well as remembering her as being naked, and so representative of the women who should be available to them, the Greeks perpetuated a troubling trope: stories abounded about Aphrodite's connection to sexual abuse.

The butter-yellow site at Palaeo Paphos back on Cyprus – in the imaginations of the ancients – concealed a rancid secret. Some said that this sanctuary was founded by a hero from the age of the Trojan War, the high priest of Aphrodite, King Kinyras. Kinyras had a daughter, Myrrha, who somehow offended the goddess. As punishment, Aphrodite cast a spell causing Kinyras' daughter to lust after her own father. As the helpless man, powerless to resist, advanced on his child, Aphrodite took pity and turned her into a myrrh (in some versions a myrtle) tree. From this tree was then born Adonis – the half-mortal shepherd boy

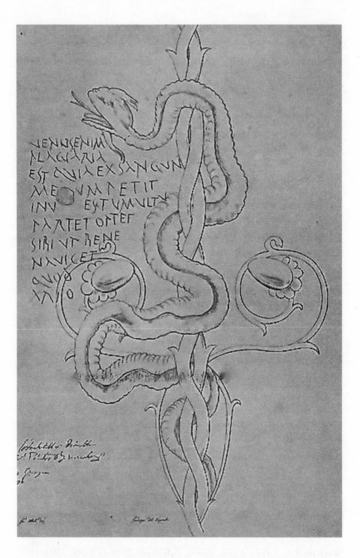

Eighteenth-century copy of a graffito in Pompeii from a
mother to her son warning of Venus, 'the weaver of webs'

who would go on to break Aphrodite's heart (a direct parallel with the Babylonian goddess Inanna's love for a mortal shepherd boy, Dumuzi). The annual Kinyras festival commemorated Kinyras' would-be incest with his daughter. It is pleasure and pain, sex and death all mixed up.

These are disturbing tales. But it was very Greek to put such horrors centre-stage. Arguably, the ancients weren't pussy-footing around the question of where desire can lead. Aphrodite was far more than just a pretty face: she was a sounding board for human behaviour and for ethical and cultural dilemmas. To the point of excess and beyond, Aphrodite-Venus was deployed as an excuse for extreme passion, extreme desire.

And the culture that harnessed the goddess's role as a driver of ravening ambition, of lust for more, and more again, was the one whose people helped to morph Aphrodite into Venus – the almighty Romans.

7

Venus & Empire
Without Limits

Venus was so named by our countrymen as the goddess who 'comes' (venire) to all things; her name is not derived from the word venustas (beauty) but rather venustas from it.[*]

---

[*] Cicero, *De Natura Deorum*, 2.69 trans. Rackham

The afterlife of Aphrodite as Venus in the Roman world reveals much about the role that desire plays in the human story. Venus was central to the Roman narrative. This is no coincidence – indeed it is critical.

The premier myth-history concerning the Roman goddess of love can be summarised thus: Aphrodite-Venus, as was her wont, enjoyed a night of passion with an attractive, bit-of-rough mortal, the Trojan shepherd Anchises. It was Anchises whom Aphrodite-Venus had pursued on Mount Ida and in the sanctuary at Paphos, and for whom she had dressed so beautifully and so odiferously (her liaison with this mere mortal was a punishment from the Olympian gods for her affair with the god of war, Mars, Ares to the Greeks). The product of this cross-species union was Aeneas, a hero of Troy who fled the devastation of the Trojan War to seek out a new home for his people. After an adventure in Carthage, where he broke the heart of the Carthaginian queen Dido, Aeneas landed in Latium (along with his son Iulus, whose name would eventually be taken by the family of Julius Caesar); Aeneas' other high-achieving descendant Romulus would famously go on to found the city of Rome.

It is during a conversation with Venus, in Book 1 of Virgil's splendid epic poem *The Aeneid*, that we hear that Aeneas' destiny was to establish – for the Roman people – an 'empire without limits'. Reading this passage amidst the ruins of the city of Carthage in modern-day Tunisia, where, over a space of six days and six nights in the second century BC, the Romans committed what would now be considered war crimes, it is still possible to feel the pulsing presence of Roman ambition in the dereliction of the ravaged stones. When it finally defeated Carthage and took over Carthage's Punic territories, Rome was on course to control the Mediterranean and to become a superpower.

Venus, with her violent origins and her choice of the war god Ares-Mars as a lover, was an appropriate deity for Rome to take up with.

The early Roman tribespeople had long worshipped a local fertility deity, Venus, a kind of homegrown Aphrodite. (Tellingly, the Sanskrit root of Venus, *vanas*, means desire and stems from a Proto-Indo-European root, *wen*, to strive for, to wish for, to desire, to love.) Venus Obsequens, indulgent Venus, was worshipped in a temple on the most southern of Rome's Seven Hills, the Aventine Hill, from around 295 BC. Interestingly enough, the historian Livy reports that this temple was paid for by a tax on women's sexual misdemeanours. And once the Romans tangled with the Greek goddess Aphrodite (and indeed the Phoenician Astarte), and as they increasingly invaded and controlled what had been Greek lands, the Latin Venus and the Grecian Aphrodite were subtly and systematically combined.

Statues of Venus and the heads and breasts of her worshippers were, like Aphrodite's, decorated with heady, sweet-smelling myrtle flowers (some in the Roman world nicknamed the female sex *myrtus* – our myrtle). During those punishing Punic Wars against the Carthaginians, a North African version of Aphrodite's Eastern grandmother, Astarte, believed by the Romans to be the Punic Venus, was captured from the mountain settlement of Eryx in Sicily and brought to Rome. A temple to this Eastern-origin Venus was set up on the Capitoline Hill. In all her forms, local and foreign, Rome wanted to claim and to control the goddess's martial powers and her compulsion for conflict. Colonisation of the domains of Aphrodite was a conscious early act in Rome's programme of global domination. Indeed, Venus became a potent ally in the Roman project.

Although her acolytes in the Greek world had

been predominantly female, in Rome Venus was a goddess for both sexes. She was honoured with four major festivals a year: the Veneralia on 1 April, as the natural world started to blossom again and when the statue of the goddess was physically given a spring-clean; the Vinalia Urbana on 22 April, when wine was drunk and prostitutes carried garlands of mint, myrtle and roses in the goddess's honour; on 19 August in a garden festival; and then, from 46 BC, on 26 September as Venus Genetrix, Venus the mother and progenitor of the Roman people. For the Romans, Venus was a goddess of both the state room and the street.

Recognising her appeal, Roman muscle-men started to develop an intimate relationship with the deity. The bellicose general Sulla chose to call himself 'the beloved of Venus' (Pompeii, don't forget, was re-established by Sulla as a protectorate of Venus). Sulla also built a temple of Venus Felix next to that of Mars Victor in the Roman capital. Another general, Pompey, invoked her name, founding sanctuaries in her honour and nominating the goddess Venus Victrix – Venus Victorious.

But it was Julius Caesar who really embraced the love-and-war goddess. Before the Battle of Pharsalus in 48 BC, Caesar and Pompey had each invoked their own Venus, asking the goddess for her unilateral support. Julius Caesar claimed his ancestral advantage, putting his name to the myth that Aphrodite had sired Aeneas, who would go on to have a son, Julius, and found the Iulii dynasty. In his funeral oration for his aunt Julia, Caesar publicly reminded the Roman world that their family was of divine descent – stemming he declared, from the primordial Julians. Subsuming Pompey's monument in the capital on 26 September 46 BC, the year he became dictator, Julius Caesar dedicated an enormous temple of Venus Genetrix in the heart of Rome, within which he erected a statue of his lover, the Egyptian queen Cleopatra VII, in the form of the goddess. Its broken columns still stand in the Forum today. At around the same time Julius Caesar started to sport a ring emblazoned with an image of Venus in warrior-dress. He had a coin minted with Venus on one side and Aeneas carrying his father Anchises on the other. Writing to the Roman orator Cicero in 49 BC, Marcus Caelius Rufus described Caesar rather mockingly as *Venere prognatus* – the spawn of Venus. And the author Cassius Dio gleefully reported that Caesar attributed the fine smoothness of his very skin to his divinely beautiful ancestor.

But Caesar had cemented Venus' imperial future. Recalling Aphrodite-Venus' martial credentials, her worship was prescribed and demanded. Subsequent Roman rulers and emperors flocked to Aphrodite's premier sanctuary at Palaeo Paphos to get blessings for vital conflicts. Temples to Venus and her lover Mars sprang up across the empire. Increasingly in Roman-period art, the goddess is represented both naked, and armed.

And as the Roman Empire expanded, so did Aphrodite-Venus' purview. At Aphrodisias in modern

Venus (Aphrodite) armed with a sword. A second century
AD statue restored in the sixteenth century. Venus flanked
by her son Cupid, who plays with her oversized helmet.
The statue belonged to the collection of Tiberio Ceuli,
now in the Louvre, Paris

A picrolite figure from Lemba, Cyprus, c.4000 BC, currently in Cyprus Museum, Nicosia

Red-breasted goddess statue – terracotta figure, c.800 BC, made in Cyprus, currently in the British Museum, London

Venus in Pompeii, reclining in a shell after her birth, accompanied by Cupid, first century AD, from the House of Venus, Pompeii, currently in the National Archaeological Museum, Naples

ABOVE RIGHT Image of the Virgin Mary, in the Catacomb of Priscilla in Rome. This is the earliest known image of Mary and the Infant Jesus independent of the Magi episode. The figure at the left appears to be the prophet Balaam pointing to a star (outside the frame), late second century AD

RIGHT Masaccio's *Expulsion of Adam and Eve from Eden*, from the Brancacci Chapel, Florence; the figure of Eve is in the stance of a Venus Pudica, 'Modest Venus', the trend initiated by the sculpture of the *Knidian Aphrodite*

Botticelli, *The Birth of Venus*, c.1485

ABOVE Fifteenth-century manuscript illumination of Venus Ourania in heaven

RIGHT Rubens's imagining of the Roman festival of Veneralia in his *Feast of Venus*, 1635/6, a work that draws on Titian's *Worship of Venus* – which itself drew inspiration from a description by Philostratus, a Greek traveller in the third century AD, of a painting in a third-century BC villa near Naples

ABOVE Tintoretto, 'Venus and Mars Surprised by Vulcan', oil on canvas, depicting Vulcan discovering, or about to discover, the affair of Venus and Mars, currently in Alte Pinakothek, Munich

ABOVE LEFT Rubens, 'Helena Fourment as Venus', oil on canvas.
Helena Fourment was said to surpass Helen of Troy in beauty

ABOVE RIGHT Exhibits in the British Museum's 2008 Statuephilia
Exhibition. The solid-gold cast of Kate Moss in a yoga pose was
made in response to 'Lely's *Venus*', the crouching Aphrodite

day Turkey – the enchanting ancient city dedicated to the goddess, on a high plateau, ringed by mountains and poplar trees – new digs consistently reveal the power of Aphrodite-Venus as an imperial ally. Worshipped here from the third century BC, probably as a synthesis with a local Anatolian mother-of-nature goddess (a winding river adjacent to the ruins keeps the land wonderfully productive), Aphrodite-Venus boasted her own substantial temple complex, a rich cult statue, the privilege of receiving an offering from the entire polis, and being honoured alongside the Divine Augusti.

The goddess is hard to escape here at Aphrodisias, famed for its marble sculptures and local marble quarry. There are stone versions of the divinity throughout: she holds a baby Eros in her lap, she stands, elegantly clothed and colossal, her tunic covered in a pounding narrative – there are intricate trees of life and an energetic deity riding a cross between a goat and a sea dragon. Elsewhere a personification of Aphrodisias is crowned by a representation of humankind, Andreia.

The hauntingly beautiful site – a humming settlement from the Hellenistic period onwards – has cogent reach. Here in the first century AD a man called Chariton, surely inspired by his surroundings, pretty much invented the novel. Chariton of Aphrodisias claimed Aphrodite as his presiding deity – and set in train two millennia worth of narratives centred on love, featuring strong female subjects. Papyrus fragments of Chariton's work are still being identified – in one historical romance, an Aphrodite-esque character Calliroe, is Chariton's lead character. And an older Aphrodite-Venus, in her iteration as a fertility goddess and nurturer of nature, is still present here in the quinces, apples and myrtle liqueurs that locals drink and share with travellers and strangers at the time of harvest.

And so the Romans, in an empire that now spanned three continents, had successfully made Aphrodite their own. Caligula, we are told by Cassius Dio, even dressed up as the goddess. His favourite sister, Drusilla, was declared a 'New Aphrodite'.

Relief of Anchises and Aphrodite,
first century AD. Anchises gazes at his lover, Aphrodite,
who holds a small Eros on her lap, from the Sebasteion,
or Augusteum, dedicated to Aphrodite. Aphrodisias
Museum, Aphrodisias, Turkey

Whether to compel or to seduce, Aphrodite-Venus was a vital part of Rome's political project, moulded to become an expression of the Roman world-view.

But the tug of love over the goddess between her new adopters, the West, and her motherland, the East, would continue – with intriguing results that still play out in our lives today.

8

Eastern Queen

*Hestiaea the grammarian says that the plain where
Aphrodite's temples stands is called Golden: that
is why it is the temple of Golden Aphrodite**

---

* Hestiaea, a female scholar and researcher of antiquity from
Alexandria is known only from four fragmentary references to
her work. She is mentioned here in the D-Scholia, a collection of
commentaries on *The Iliad* dating from between the fifth centuries
BC to the seventh centuries AD, and cited by medieval scholars

North Africa and the Middle East, Egypt in particular, had never forgotten their love of the love goddess.

From the Ptolemaic period onwards, Aphrodite-Venus had become a hugely popular deity in Alexandria on Egypt's Mediterranean coast. Walking the Alexandrian corniche today, under the drama of a winter electric storm or in the brilliance of summer heat, it is easy to imagine how Aphrodite-Venus was cherished as a patron of this cross-border, cross-boundary, headily ambitious and cosmopolitan city.

The goddess Isis had been adored here by the Ancient Egyptians and, come the reconfiguring of the city by Alexander the Great and his successors, her cult spaces were frequently modified so the Egyptian goddess came to look more like a Greek Aphrodite. Excavations at the nearby town of Naukratis (the home town of Athenaeus, one of our go-to sources for Aphrodite's life story), just inland from Alexandria, show how seriously devotees invested in Aphrodite worship. One of the richest traders from one of the richest trading families in the Mediterranean, Sostratos of Aegina, dedicated to the goddess a beautiful bowl made on the Eastern Mediterranean island of Chios. A poorer pilgrim gave her a typical Egyptian offering spoon. We get a wonderful insight into the real passion with which she was adored thanks to a certain Herostratos, a trader based on the North African coast, who, having picked up a statuette of Aphrodite from Alexandria on a round trip to Paphos in Cyprus, and weathering a life-threatening storm with the help of the goddess, brought the figurine back to dedicate to Aphrodite and then invited 'his relations and closest friends to a feast in her temple'. Sheep, goats or pigs would have been slaughtered and plenty of wine drunk. Eyewitnesses even reported, in the city's great festival of Ptolemaia, which celebrated the Ptolemies' royal succession, a 120-foot-wide, gem-encrusted myrtle wreath (representing both the goddess and female genitalia) accompanied by an eighty-foot-long gold, star-tipped phallus being paraded along the streets in Aphrodite's honour.

A statue of the goddess was recently rescued from the nearby waters at Canopus. This is officially an image of the Ptolemaic queen Arsinoe II, but in the guise of the goddess of love. The underwater find is an extraordinary thing. Close up, you can see the stone has been buffed to a satin sheen. Made of black granodiorite, the cloth is sculpted to appear wet – clinging enticingly to the divine queen's lovely, taut body beneath. The sculpture's nipples are just visible above the damp shift. For the regal goddess who saw sailors home safely to port and also protected the prostitutes they would meet when they arrived, this Aphrodite is a predictably fitting fantasy.

We find figurines of Aphrodite-Venus identified in the dowries of well-to-do young Alexandrian girls. No fewer than twenty-one cities bear her name across Upper and Lower Egypt. And Cleopatra VII, Arsinoe's descendant – who called Alexandria her home – actively exploited the connection between herself and this deity who was sex and power incarnate. Identifying as a combination of the Greco-Roman goddess and the Egyptian Isis, the Egyptian queen styled herself a living Venus, wearing golden sandals and heavy perfumes, and with coils of auburn-gold hair tendrilling down her neck. (This fashion would become so popular that a number of Roman women would mimic it – gruesomely, using hair-pieces created from the hair of captured Germanic slaves.) A tantalising papyrus now kept in Berlin even suggests that Cleopatra was worshipped at some locations in Egypt as Aphrodite-Venus herself.

Cleopatra had visited the new Temple of Venus Genetrix in Rome, featuring the Egyptian queen in divine, sculptural form, when she took her son Caesarion to meet his father Caesar. And when she moved on to her next Roman lover, Marc Antony, we are told she dressed as the goddess to meet the pleasure-loving, party-animal general in Tarsus in modern-day Turkey – an Aphrodite-Venus to his Dionysos-Bacchus. Sailing up the River Kydnos, she must have made quite an impact:

> in a gold-prowed barge with purple sails spread,
> rowed along by silver oars to the sound of the
> flute mingled with pipes. She [Cleopatra] lay
> beneath a gold-spangled canopy, adorned like
> Aphrodite in a picture, and young boys, like
> Cupids, stood on either side and fanned her. The
> most beautiful of her serving maids, wearing the
> robes of the Nereids and of Graces, stood by the
> bulwarks. Wonderful scents from many types
> of incense permeated the river banks. Some of
> the populus escorted her on either side from the

river mouth and others came down from the city

for the spectacle. The crowd in the market-place

poured out, until Antony himself, seated on his

*tribunal seat, was left alone.**

This was a political statement – but also a homage to the sensuousness and pleasure Aphrodite-Venus patronised in seduction and in physical love. Strategically, Cleopatra refused to leave the barge to meet Marc Antony; he had to come to her. He could not resist the dare, and the most celebrated love affair in ancient history began.

Indeed, once their love was consummated, Cleopatra was given the island of Cyprus as a love-token by Marc Antony thanks to its association with the goddess. In Cyprus we can see the Roman-period mosaics that Cleopatra could have walked upon, a number of which picture Aphrodite-Venus: Aphrodite bathing, Aphrodite armed, the story of Leda and the

---

* Plutarch, *Antony*, 26, ed. Rowlandson

Swan – the Spartan queen Leda's doomed love that will conceive Helen and then, thanks to the power of lust and desire, spark the world-shaping Trojan War. The Roman-period site of Nea Paphos (or New Paphos) developed a thriving tourist trade as an Aphrodite-Venus-themed destination. Comfortable accommodation was available to those who wished to visit the nearby sanctuary of Palaeo Paphos and to pay their respects to the goddess, already by this time thousands of years old.

So Aphrodite was still an expression of power, a mark of physical and metaphysical might. It was with good reason that the Ptolemeies' state barge on the Nile also contained a domed shrine to, and statue of, Aphrodite. But then we see a subtle shift. Once Cleopatra and her lover Marc Antony were dead, young Octavian, soon to be Emperor Augustus, took over Rome's territories and her moral timbre too.

On coins and in statue form he increasingly represented himself as a man of both bounty and high morals. Through the Augustan period, images of Venus became the fashionable decoration of the well-to-do Roman home – imperial branding telling Rome's growing citizen-body that they were living in a pleasure-filled 'Golden Age'. But although Augustus maintained the Venus cult, her naked images appeared increasingly in private quarters, decorating dining rooms, bath rooms, bath houses. I've had the good fortune to hold one example, a delicate fresco fragment. Lovely, lightly coloured, it is full of movement and promise. Aphrodite-Venus was coming to represent something which should, by rights, be kept under wraps – the hedonistic possibilities of *tryphé*, the luxurious good life.

*

At Petra in Jordan, once the haunt of Astarte, a fine and sensual statue of Venus has recently been found. In the mesmeric landscape, in the city built by the Nabateans and then occupied by the Romans, the white limestone of the goddess glints from the beautiful burr of the ruddy sandstone. Bedouin boys rock past on camels or race by on horses and donkeys. Discovered on the northern Petran ridge, this Aphrodite-Venus is a bit of a mystery. She is naked, her hair piled high in an elaborate coiffure; why was this nude goddess found next to the stairs in a relatively modest home? Consistently adored in this Roman province, then called Arabia, in conjunction with Dionysos-Bacchus, the luscious lady once again ended up in a domestic setting, mirroring perhaps the use of miniaturised Venuses in the homes of the people of Pompeii – Romans proving they appreciated the art and culture of the 'ancient' Greeks who had gone before them.

Another Aphrodite-Venus statue has recently been discovered at the site of Jerash, close to Jordan's northern border with Syria. And there are more finds still to come. One of the artefacts recently rescued from the illegal antiquities trade, looted by the foot soldiers of ISIS, is a mournful Aphrodite-Venus head: a goddess who once represented war, decapitated by the blind passions of holy warfare and then knowingly traded for cash. The fact that retrieved Venus and Aphrodite artefacts stolen by ISIS originated in Syria, Libya and Yemen is a perverse indication of the goddess's reach.

Even though Venus might have been becoming, in some Roman quarters, more than a little like a glamour model, her throbbing, primal power had not yet fully diminished. When the Roman author Tacitus reported on a visit of the emperor Titus to Aphrodite's shrine at Palaeo Paphos in the early first century AD, he was horrified to have to bear witness to a large stone cone, twilight-grey but painted white, representing the goddess, a stone that was rubbed with olive oil. An igneous boulder was discovered near the site in the nineteenth century and was swiftly claimed to be 'Aphrodite's Rock' – travellers still visit it with some curiosity today. A coin minted around the time of Tacitus' account also shows the goddess in the guise of a megalith. There are records in the sanctuary of stones being dressed with flowers and adored – a primitive remnant of a fertility cult. These baetyl stones (which probably did represent the prehistoric goddess) can be found elsewhere on Cyprus in her Bronze Age sanctuaries. As Tacitus puts it with curiosity verging on distaste, 'the origins of the goddess in this form are obscure'.* The worship of Aphrodite has long brought with it something sinister, more than a little menace.

It was with good reason that the emperor Hadrian built a temple to Venus at Golgotha – the Place of the Skulls – in Jerusalem, matching that which he had built for Venus and Roma Aeterna on the Velian Hill in Rome in AD 135. Hadrian was specifically using Venus' dark magic to drown out the resonance of the cave where the Jewish rebel Jesus had been buried.

So, despite Augustus' best efforts, back in her Eastern homeland and across central and southern

---

* Tacitus, *Histories*, 2.3

Europe Aphrodite-Venus appeared to be ruling confidently. But there was trouble ahead, in the form of a peace-preaching, desire-adverse boy-god.

9

Venus in Middle Age

*I will sing of stately Aphrodite, gold-crowned and
beautiful, whose dominion is the walled cities**

*Nearby shone Kypris, shedding drops of beauty
on the bright bronze. She appeared bare-breasted,
gathering a robe about her rounded thighs, her
locks bound with a golden veil ... I saw another
high-born golden Aphrodite, naked and radiant.
Upon her breasts, hanging from her neck, fell in
coils her flowing girdle ... I was again amazed at
the third golden Aphrodite, her hips shaded by a
cloak. Her twisted girdle hung loosely about her
breasts, and in that girdle her beauty floated.*†

---

* *Homeric Hymn* 6.1–3, trans. Evelyn-White
† Christodoros of Egypt describing the sculptures of Aphrodite
in the Baths of Zeuxippos in the Christian city of Constantinople,
The Greek Anthology 2. 78–80, 99–101, 288–290, trans. Paton

Pagans, men and women, bearing the statue of
Kypris with torches and incense burners, passed
near the holy church in blatant pagan delirium
and dancing. When the saint heard them, he went
out, with his clergy men, broke the idol and made
them ashamed ...[*]

* *The Life of St Tychon*, by Saint John the Almsgiver, 60.3, trans. Usener

The hilltop city of Madaba in Jordan is famous for its mosaics. Ancient and modern visitors alike have flocked there to marvel at what is declared to be the oldest stone map in the world. Dating to as early as AD 542, orientating not north but east, the Madaba Map depicts the hot spots of Christendom and is centred on the Byzantine emperor Justinian I's church dedicated in Jerusalem to Mary Theotokos – Mary the Mother of God.

But there's another, rather more neglected, mosaic in this lively, traditional little town that is of equal interest. It can be found slap-bang under a Christian church. To reach this gem you have to walk down narrow side streets. Jordanian guards are pleasantly surprised by the atypical attention. And there, at the back of a courtyard where cats sunbathe, is a compelling iteration of the goddess of love. Spreading across the floor, a plump and perky Aphrodite sits with her mortal lover Adonis. An overturned beehive reminds the viewer of both the sweet honey of sex and its sting. For centuries all that ebullient, edgy joy was hidden. Because time and time again, the Christian revolution recognised Aphrodite-Venus' pulling power and so moved into her temporal homes, attempting to suppress or morph her memory by constructing their new houses of worship full-square on top of her shrines.

Now, you would expect the goddess of desire and conflict and sexual love to fare extremely badly as the new Christ cult took hold. Aphrodite-Venus was certainly the focus of much ire. One of the leading Church Fathers, Clement of Alexandria, wrote with disgust of Aphrodite-worship, particularly the cult of

Aphrodite of the Beautiful Buttocks. In Athens one of her prominent sculptures was desecrated, scored across the forehead with a rough cross. Her nipples, sculpted so convincingly by one man's careful hands, were gouged out by many. A statue of the goddess from Memphis in Egypt was bundled on to the back of a camel, pounded along the long desert road to the northern coast at Alexandria, and then publicly ridiculed in the city where she had once held sway.

In Lebanon's Beqaa Valley, at Baalbek, beyond the Green Zone, today blatantly populated by opium warlords and their militias, stood Aphrodite's lovely little grotto-shaped temple – a building of curves – also described as a nymphaeum. First built by the African emperor Septimius Severus, the temple was shut down by Constantine the Great. Originally dedicated to Astarte, there is little left of the delicate structure today – just the back end, rather like the last, crumbling slice of a wedding cake. The Church chronicler Eusebius of Caesarea reported with horror that sacred prostitution was practised here: 'men and women vie with one another to honour their shameless goddess; husbands and fathers let their wives and daughters publicly prostitute themselves to please Astarte!' * But Aphrodite's hangout was too charming a building not to use; it was turned into a church and eventually dedicated to a local saint, St Barbara. Today it sits as a fenced-off ruin, with local hawkers selling postcards, or something stronger, to the few visitors who pass by.

And across the newly Christian Roman Empire, temples to Aphrodite were being converted into chapels. At that rich city of Aphrodisias, the splendid Temple of Aphrodite was physically turned inside out and back to front to become the splendid basilica of St Michael. The Bishop of Jerusalem was an ally in the empire-wide rebuilding programme. In order to locate the exact spot of Jesus' crucifixion, the sanctuary of 'that impure demon called Aphrodite, a dark shrine of

---

* Eusebius, *Life of Constantine*, 3.55

lifeless idols' was demolished. In Corinth, the temple once teeming with holy whores was made a shrine for the Holy Ghost. Frequently built over or near springs, Aphrodite's temple locations were now believed to give succour and sustain life in a new way, with a new spiritual gloss.

But despite their official disgrace, statues of Aphrodite could still be found in the very heartlands of Christendom – in particular in the city of Constantinople, the headquarters of Constantine the Great that would be rebranded the New Rome. In Constantinople the powerful Christian eunuch Lausos, the great chamberlain to the emperor, collected up the beautiful *Knidian Aphrodite* for loving display. Sadly, hers would be a brief visit: the statue was lost along with many other world-class antiquities when Lausos' palace and library burnt down in AD 475. Up until the time of the Fourth Crusade, when, in 1204, the city was put to the torch by ravaging crusader knights, a bronze Aphrodite had proudly stood outside the Senate House in the political heart of the city. Her images still decorated the famous baths of the capital, and indeed baths across the empire. Women – even the female relatives of Byzantine emperors – paraded in front of one of these on Zeugma Hill to test whether or not they were adulteresses (one particular aristocrat, sister-in-law to Emperor Justin II, was revealed to be unchaste; the tell-tale statue was subsequently hastily torn down). So some Aphrodite-Venuses survived the spiritual revolution of Christianity, and many sculptures were still believed to possess and ooze a kind of demonic power; but faith-fuelled destruction was more common.

From the fifth century onwards images of the goddess were smashed, burnt and felled with dogmatic gusto. Mark the Deacon described Bishop Porphyry of Gaza's elimination, together with a Christian mob, of one Venus who stood on an altar in Porphyry's bishopric. Mark commented that the violence of Aphrodite's demise could be explained by the fact that local women asked the Venetic marriage idol for advice and then wed their beaux, but were often disappointed later in life with a bitter divorce.

Aphrodite's reputation was also corrupted in literary texts. The Christian author Colluthus, from the lovely town of Lycopolis on the banks of the Nile, writing in the late fifth and early sixth centuries overtly sexualised the fragrant Aphrodite who had travelled to Mount Ida in preparation for the Judgement of Paris. He tells us that the goddess 'lifted up her deep-bosomed robe and bared her breast to the air and had no shame. And lifting with her hands the honeyed girdle of many Loves she bared her bosom and heeded not her breasts.' *

Incidentally, Colluthus' verdant riverbank hometown is still deeply religious. It was said – in fact, has been confirmed by the Coptic Orthodox Church – that the Virgin Mary appeared there in the year 2000.

---

* Colluthus, *Rape of Helen*, 115–8, trans. Mair

But a 4,000-year-old goddess is hard to dethrone overnight. Aphrodite was not destroyed, she simply shape-shifted once more. Astarte-Aphrodite-Venus' tenacity across the four millennia before the birth of Christ demonstrated that humans wanted the comfort and stimulation of a strong, sympathetic, female presence as an intercessor with the supernatural world. So, counter-intuitively, in the monotheistic climate of Christendom, Aphrodite survived a faith revolution – in no less a guise than the Virgin Mary herself.

If you make your way up to the Troodos mountain range in central Cyprus, through leafy plane trees, there is the opportunity to meet a priest at the Monastery of the Panagia Trooditissa who will proudly show the many letters of thanks that he has been sent by grateful women. Father Efthymios' secret? Behind the altar frieze there is a silver belt, said to have been blessed by the Virgin Mary, which some believe has life-giving powers. The celibate man of God – gentle, offering homemade pickled walnuts, mobile phone to hand – is very clear that this is not a magic belt. But he is also clear that it – or the power of prayer that it encourages – is effective. Dating back to the ninth century, this monastery is also known as the Monastery of Panagia Aphroditissa; the whole mountainside was once sacred to Aphrodite Akraia, Aphrodite of the High Mountains. The relic here is remarkably similar to Aphrodite's girdle of mythology – her ornate *kestos himas* – behind which was contained all her power, the power of love – a magic belt indeed.

Mary's girdle, medieval authors recalled, was dropped en route to heaven to prove to doubting Thomas that the Assumption was indeed taking place. And another of Aphrodite's favourites, the dove, was a companion of Mary, only this time at the Annunciation. Frescoes in Mount Athos, in Syria and in Cyprus also show Mary breastfeeding Jesus with the 'milk of paradise'. The equation between Aphrodite as a nurturer or protector of children, a *kourotrophos*, and the Virgin Mary is obvious.

Another Christian church, dedicated to All-Holy Mary, the Church of Panagia Katholiki, was built in the centre of Aphrodite's precinct at Palaeo Paphos in the twelfth century. Old women with health issues or young women with fertility problems still go there to make small offerings at the pagan stones used to build the Orthodox church: cups of milk, pomegranates, little cakes. Their votive gifts are strikingly similar to those from votaries who came here to worship the goddess over 3,000 years before.

In many ways, particularly in the East, Mary of Nazareth was the ancient, teenage, mother goddess – her face unchanged – enjoying an outing in new clothes: the medieval population of Christendom did not want to risk losing contact with a sublime female creature whose powers of cohesion and union were becoming ever more relevant.

Aphrodite as guardian of Constantinople on the Peutinger
Map, a thirteenth-century copy of the Roman original,
commissioned by Emperor Augustus in the first century BC
and revised in the fourth century AD

✳

Aphrodite-Venus' prehistoric, Eastern ancestors emerged as cities were becoming a defining feature of civilisation itself. Aphrodite had, since the classical period, been adored as the goddess of *harmonia* and *homonia*, concord and union. And through antiquity and beyond, she was consistently and widely considered a protector of urban cultures. This was the deity, don't forget, who encouraged men and women to live together.

Aphrodite was believed to be, along with Athena, a great protector of the city of Athens – a 'blue-print' city for Western civilisation. The goddess was honoured in the Agora at Athens, where an impressive number of goats, judging from the bone remains found, were sacrificed in front of her brightly painted altar. As Aphrodite Pandemos, Aphrodite of All People, she was twinned with Peitho, the goddess of persuasion (in a direct democracy a lot of persuading needed to happen to keep all those citizen-democrats happily getting along and doing politics with one another), and she was believed to inhabit her shrine just under the entrance to the Parthenon. Here the tongues of doves would be torn out as a (relatively) delicate sacrifice to the goddess. Along the sacred way towards Eleusis at Daphni, its pastoral peace now spoilt by a six-lane highway, the goddess was again worshipped with the dedication of doves; a shrine to Mary's Dormition stands where Aphrodite once reigned. Pausanias tells us that in Athens there was a garden sanctuary to Aphrodite en Kepois by the cool banks of the River Ilissos, and another to Ourania – Heavenly Aphrodite.

The north slope of Athens' Acropolis itself was sacred to the goddess. Young girls would wind their way up through a Bronze Age staircase within the very rock bringing, Pausanias tells us, 'unspeakable things'* in baskets in honour of the deity. The

---

* Pausanias, *Description of Greece* 1.27.3

staircase still exists, although investigation is not allowed or advised as it is perilous, and thick with the guano of bats and the excrement of Aphrodite's sacred bird. Today, on narrow pathways around the red-granite rock faces of the Acropolis, those both lucky and unlucky in love still leave offerings of pomegranates – Aphrodite's fruit – to her spirit. Then and now the goddess enjoys the very best views in the city. It was said that protecting-Aphrodite – with her maritime connections – had even metamorphosed into a dove and led the flagship of the Athenian general Themistocles to victory over the Persians at the Battle of Salamis in 480 BC.

On the extraordinary Peutinger Map, first ordered by Augustus to map the Roman Empire and then copied and reproduced down time, it is Aphrodite who safeguards the great city of Constantinople, modern-day Istanbul. Recent digs in the city – as new road and rail tunnels are being carved out under the Bosphorus – have revealed a sanctuary where women are buried with a pierced oyster or scallop shell, a symbol of Aphrodite's worship since prehistory. The goddess had been given charge of one of the greatest and most influential metropolises on earth, a city that was a bridge between East and West, North and South, and that was affectionately named the Queen of Cities, and the World's Desire.

In both antiquity and the medieval world Aphrodite-Venus was a sustained presence in great and small ways: as an idea – as a notion of concord, in high politics and high culture – and on the dressing tables of ordinary women and men. The huge number of surviving ivory, silver and gold decorations from the fourth to fourteenth centuries AD tell us that the image of Aphrodite bathing, slipping on her sandal, or combing her hair was hugely popular. She wasn't just a pin-up, she was a decorative pin on cosmetic boxes and marriage gifts.

So, the drive to create, and to mate, and to make war – all urges wrapped into the figure of

Aphrodite-Venus and her ancestors – helped to kick-start civilisation in the Bronze Age. Across time her protective and unifying spirit was credited with keeping prehistoric, ancient and medieval cities (and citizens) cohesive. Four thousand years later the notion of the goddess, in pen and ink, in stone, in silver and ivory and vellum, in poetry, prose and even prayer, was a quiet witness to the creations not just of the hand and heart, but of the medieval mind. Because Aphrodite-Venus was about to become a metaphor, no longer for ambition and for prurient passion, but for purist philosophy.

10

A Humanist Muse

We read there are indeed two Venuses,
One lawful, and the other the goddess of lust.
The lawful Venus is the harmony of the world ...
The shameless Venus, however,
The goddess of lust, is carnal concupiscence,
Which is the mother of all fornications.*

---

* Bernardus Silvestris, *Commentary on the First Six Books of the Aeneid of Vergil*, 'On Book 1', trans. Maresca and Schreiber

There were some who wanted to forget about the material, the carnal, all that hot sex and see the pure, the high-minded, the spiritual beauty in the goddess. Aphrodite became an unlikely ally in the cause of Renaissance philosophy.

After the fall of Constantinople to Ottoman forces in 1453, Greek manuscripts, including those containing the heady *Homeric Hymns to Aphrodite*, arrived in Italy. Galvanised, many more now wanted not just to own a bit of classical art, but to understand and advance it. Classics consultancy started to boom. The Medici patrons of Botticelli, for example, employed the philosopher-poet-translator Poliziano and the family

Botticelli, *Venus and Mars*, c.1485–88.
Tempera and oil on poplar panel, currently
in the National Gallery, London

tutor and philosophy expert Marsilio Ficino. While some approached their task with a scholarly rigour (for example Georg Pictor, who in his *Mythological Theology* of 1532 fascinatingly recorded the Latin author Macrobius' assertion that a Venus with a beard and a penis existed on Cyprus and that cross-dressing men and women would sacrifice to this bi-gendered deity), others took a more abstract line. Ficino's Neoplatonic approach was to encourage his clients to see complex messages and meaning in simple material things. For instance, the viewing of a painting would inspire a ladder of ideas, each visual detail a step leading up to a higher spiritual plane.

Botticelli's *Venus and Mars* does exactly that. Venus here represents the 'feminine' virtues of grace and beauty, overcoming the destructive, uber-male passions of Mars, the god of war. Like many Renaissance images that we now view in the lionising setting of a gallery, *Venus and Mars* was almost certainly originally a headboard for a bed – probably for newly-weds. The twigs of myrtle behind Venus signify to us that this is indeed the goddess, and a goddess dominant over her lover: as Ficino saw it, even in astrology 'Venus dominates Mars, never vice versa'. The presence of bestial satyrs recalled the dangers of lust polluting spiritual love. The thorn apple – a member of the deadly-nightshade family and with a similar effect to opiates – held by one trouble-making satyr hiding under Mars' polished cuirass reminded those in the bed of the intoxicating effects of desire. (Bizarrely, one effect of eating this particular fruit is apparently to tempt the user to remove her/his clothing.) Venus had become a player in an elite, intellectual, pictorial game – albeit one with a political touch.

Commissioned, almost certainly, to celebrate the (arranged) marriage of Lorenzo de Medici's daughter Lucrezia to a young man from a rival Florentine family, the Salviati – who had recently been involved in a conspiracy against the Medici – the creation of *Venus and Mars* was a political move. If Venus, elegantly clothed on this canvas, represented the higher magnanimity of peace, the naked, unprincipled Mars was subtly recalling a lower-rank (exposed and vulnerable) member of the pugilistic Salviati clan.

Non-religious paintings were flourishing in Renaissance Italy. They became so popular that the choleric priest Savonarola famously commanded the destruction of many during the Florence carnival in his Bonfire of the Vanities in 1493. Venus was a particular focus of his ire: 'As for the houses of the citizens, what can I say?' Savonarola trumpeted. 'No merchant's daughter enters a marriage without a trousseau painted with pagan stories. The newly-wed Christian woman is more likely to know about the infidelities of Mars [with Venus] than about the saintly women of the Bible!' *

But Venus could not be censored so easily.

---

* Savonarola, Ruth and Micheas, Sermon XXVIII

Botticelli went on to paint the goddess's remarkable arrival on the island of Cyprus; this artwork, *The Birth of Venus*, completed sometime between 1484 and 1486, would have a lasting impact on global culture and ideas.

Featuring the first life-size naked painting of a woman in the Western canon, *The Birth of Venus* would go on to be referenced, copied, parodied and marketed right up to the present day. Botticelli's Renaissance goddess luxuriates in classical context. One of Venus' companions wears a girdle of myrtle, erect bulrushes represent the charged eroticism of the Ouranos-Gaia story, the soft-red cloak and roses are an elegant nod to the gory mass of castrated matter from which Aphrodite was said to have emerged.

The Birth of Venus also acknowledges the ancients because it was art painted to stimulate; to immortalise and communicate ideas. It is a hymn to beauty, physical and metaphysical. Along with works by Bronzino,

Cranach, Holbein, Jan Massys et al., Renaissance art inspired by classical allegory demonstrated that Neoplatonic perfection can be made incarnate in what is sublime on earth. The Greek philosopher Plotinus, whose steer was eagerly followed, opined in his *Enneads I*: 'This is the spirit that Beauty must ever induce: wonderment and a delicious trouble, longing and love and a trembling that is all delight.' In paintings that were eagerly commissioned and then carefully installed behind the heavy doors of merchants and nobles in Renaissance villas, Venus' immortality was secured in gaudy, one-dimensional form.

And the goddess was still there on the streets too. Adventuring knights and crusaders had brought back Eastern poetry forms and lyrics which troubadour singer-songwriters then turned into love songs for the late-medieval world. 'The First Troubadour' William IX, Duke of Aquitaine and Gascony, had in fact inherited, age fifteen, a consignment of singing girls originally from Muslim households following the earlier fall of the Islamic-Iberian city of Barbastro in 1064. The work of these unfortunate women, who were trained in end-rhyme, appears to have transformed Western music. Traditionally singing of love as a welcome malady, and commemorating the pangs of the lover, a number of the new Western ballads (which would go on to influence modern pop songs) played on classical themes – statues of Venus or the Virgin Mary that came to life and demanded absolute devotion from young men. There were exhortations in these chansons to avoid the 'Bad Venus' and seek the 'Good Venus' in a woman. The hallmark of a beautiful lady, in troubadour terms, was being a mystical female partner in a relationship, superficially dominant while ultimately satisfying her male lover's wishes. Ideas of Venetic desire were strummed and sung on cobbled streets and squares throughout Northern and Southern Europe in the medieval period and Renaissance, as well as adorning the richest homes in Western civilisation.

*

Treasured in its day, much of Botticelli's canon was subsequently neglected until Emperor Napoleon Bonaparte's grand, Europe-wide secularisation project 300 years later, when a number of artworks were released from religious institutions and dispersed on to the art market. Inspiring Pre-Raphaelites from Sir John Everett Millais onwards, Botticelli's Venus became a cultural touchstone. In 1887 Debussy composed his suite *Printemps* with Botticelli in mind; in 1902 Isadora Duncan performed 'La Primavera' – she claimed to have been born under the star of Aphrodite and the goddess was a returning fixture in her repertoire; Ursula Andress emerged from the sea with shells in the 1962 film *Dr No* and Andy Warhol turned Venus into technicolour pop art. Recent research by the neuroscientists Tomohiro Ishizu and Semir Zeki, who have formulated a 'brain-based theory of beauty', identified *The Birth of Venus* as one of the ten most beautiful paintings in the world.

Despite her vicissitudes in late antiquity and the early medieval period, despite being outlawed and banished and condemned, Venus had become a Venus Victrix once more, a symbol of beauty and love conquering the dark urges of longing and lust. She was proving herself irresistible, and as a favoured object of desire and contemplation was set to be vigorously exploited by the modern world for material gain.

11

Venus at the Box Office

Venus in Furs has caught his soul in the red snares of hair. He will paint her, and go mad.[*]

---

[*] Leopold von Sacher-Masoch, *Venus in Furs*, trans. Savage

Aphrodite-Venus is not just tenacious, she is good box office. And one aspiring author in sixteenth-century England – William Shakespeare – recognised precisely that.

Shakespeare's popular, raunchy, narrative poem *Venus and Adonis*, his first published work, was reprinted no fewer than six times in as many years. Written in 1593 – possibly out of desperation to make some cash after the theatres of London had been closed because of an outbreak of the plague the year before – this work of verse was quietly subversive. While dealing with the psychological impact of love versus lust, it features a muscular, perspiring, somewhat dominatrix

Venus who hunts down a rather woebegone Adonis. She is a 'sick-thoughted Venus', a woman consumed by desire. It was all, perhaps, a clever, quiet dig at Shakespeare's queen, the elderly Elizabeth I, a female ruler in a world dominated by men.

Inspired by Book 10 of Ovid's *Metamorphoses*, which Shakespeare, like so many schoolboys of his day would have read in the 1567 translation of Arthur Golding, in *Venus and Adonis* the goddess hunts naked, she ravens for Adonis, and in pretty explicit terms offers herself to him. The story then plays out as it has done in some versions since antiquity: Adonis is gored by a wild boar and dies. The huntsman is hunted down. The ground, stained red with Adonis' blood, bursts bright with anemone flowers. The writing is super-suggestive. Despite the fact there were sixteen editions within fifty years, hardly any original copies have survived: scholars think the imprints were so thoroughly and ardently thumbed that most have simply fallen apart.

Titian, *Venus Anadyomene*, *c.*1520. Oil on canvas,
currently in the Scottish National Gallery, Edinburgh

Shakespeare went on to reference Venus throughout his work. He describes Cleopatra as a Venus and acknowledges the goddess's romantic power in A *Midsummer Night's Dream*. But the bard's goddess often has a malicious, capricious edge. Claudio, in Act Four of *Much Ado About Nothing*, says of Hero: 'you are more intemperate in your blood / Than Venus'. Mercutio references a 'gossip Venus' in Act Two of *Romeo and Juliet*. In *As You Like It*, Act Four, it is the progeny of Venus that comes under fire. Orlando is called a 'wicked bastard of Venus, that was begot of thought, conceived of spleen, and born of madness, that blind rascally boy that abuses everyone's eyes'.

✳

Shakespeare, who frequently looked both back in time and geographically East for inspiration, may well have been aware of Venus' fashionable, and profitable, popularity in the voguish city of Venice. Because Venus and Venice were developing a particularly strong relationship. As the Venetians grew politically and commercially more powerful, they consciously developed Venetian foundation myths which crowbarred in the goddess. The Venetians declared that theirs was an ancient city (Venice was founded sometime around the fifth century AD); that their birth from the salty waters of the sea – like Venus' – was magical; that as dwellers in one of the most beautiful cities on earth they had the sublime spirit of the goddess in them; and that the name Venice stems from Venus (it derives, in fact, from the ancient Veneti tribe). The goddess was being put to work once again, in new ways.

Aphrodite-Venus (ironically, given her Eastern origins) also came to represent a sectarian, Western, Catholic ideal, set in direct contrast with the 'barbarism' of the East. The commander of the papal

Jacopo Pesaro being presented by
Pope Alexander VI to St Peter, *c.*1506–11.
Note the naked Venus on St Peter's throne.
Titian, oil on canvas, currently in
the Royal Museum of Fine Arts, Antwerp

fleet, Jacopo Pesaro (additionally, as it happened, an absentee Bishop of Paphos on Cyprus), commissioned the Venetian artist Titian to paint a celebratory work that commemorated his victory over the Ottomans at the island of Lefkada.

On the canvas, the base of St Peter's throne, no less, is decorated with a nude image of Venus in the Venus Victrix pose – as the goddess of virtuous, righteous love triumphing over the degraded enemy. When Venice took control of Cyprus – that lynchpin trading hub between three continents, and a bulwark against the Ottoman Empire – Venetians commemorated their victory by immortalising Venus (as Cyprus) in marble at the foot of the bell-tower in St Mark's Square. The relief is still in situ today, a convenient perch for pigeons and occasionally the doves long associated with the goddess.

High-ranking Venetians posted to the new colony of Cyprus excitedly declared that they had discovered the actual tomb of Venus in various locations on the island. One porphyry sarcophagus in the Cathedral of St Sophia in Nicosia – said to have been heaved from the mountains of Scythia by Mars for his paramour – was subsequently requested as the burial place for King James II Lusignan. Venus was becoming not an immortal Olympian, but a flesh-and-blood, Western European matriarch. Owning Venus, her accoutrements and her name, was starting to really matter once again in both material and political terms.

No surprise then, perhaps, that we find Venus frequently appearing in the works of Titian. Inspired by a corrupted version of Ovid's work, the Venetian paints slick after oil slick of voluptuous flesh depicting the goddess in various legendary guises: Venus emerging from the sea, Venus staring unabashed from a rich-red couch, Venus with an organist and Cupid, Venus holding roses and caressing her genitals. It was in Venice that the daring fashion for artists to depict the naked goddess tauntingly reclining took hold. In

Titian, *Venus of Urbino*, *c*.1534. Oil on canvas,
currently in the Uffizi Gallery, Florence

fact, the Venus who appeared in oil on canvas in the salons of the West was now very rarely clothed. She was instead a perfect woman, perfectly plump, waiting to be enjoyed.

Increasingly this ancient, omnipotent deity was held up as a model mortal, an impossible ideal to be emulated by the flesh-and-blood women of the early modern age.

One French doctor of the sixteenth century, Louis Guyon, in his *Le Miroir de la Beauté* went so far as to prescribe his 'succinct description of bodily beauty' for living, breathing females – which, he advised, should be judged unclothed, just as Aphrodite-Venus had stood naked in front of Paris during his Judgement. A woman's hair, Guyon opines, should be blonde, her neck long, her eyes shining, her breasts firm and neither too small nor too big – a bit like apples. Hips should be shapely and stomachs a little plump, but not wrinkled. Thighs, buttocks, arms should all be ample. This paragon female body takes its cue from the classical and Renaissance statues of Venus. The women of the time were not afforded the power of a goddess, but they were expected to look like one. In Venice in 1555 the *Secreti del reverendo donno Alessio Piemontese* was published and was translated into virtually all European languages and reissued in over ninety editions. This advanced the theme and contained recipes that encouraged women to achieve physical perfection: hair-removal creams, hair dyes, anti-wrinkle lotions, milk, sugar and butter to make the body sleek and Venus-like.

Meanwhile, on the stage, Venus was being paraded as an excuse for contemplation, and sometimes titillation. The popular opera *Venus and Adonis*, composed by John Blow with a libretto by Anne Kingsmill, was first performed to great acclaim in 1683. In the London premier the goddess was played by one of Charles II's discarded mistresses, Moll Davies. Energetic, sexy (despite the fact that Blow was the Chapel Royal's composer), richly costumed, this creation was quite a sight. Although Blow's *Venus and Adonis* was arguably the first-ever English opera, it was also the last ever royal English masque. This theatrical Venus was the culmination of a centuries-long tradition. The goddess was no stranger to the limelight; she was, rather, a character in dramas of many kinds; even back in the Roman period Venus had appeared centre-stage, in the arena.

One intriguing piece of evidence for Venus' long thespian career comes from Mactar in modern-day central Tunisia, a remarkable site still dominated by an enormous triumphal arch of Trajan. I last visited Mactar in winter, when white flowers scattered the vast stretches of green. This was once a thriving town, originally settled by Punic refugees escaping Rome's destruction of the Carthaginian superpower. Rebel locals had gradually bought into the Roman project. Come late antiquity and Mactar (another city, incidentally, featured on the wonderful Peutinger Map) was as Roman as Roman cities come. An amphitheatre enjoyed a rocking trade here, and half a day's ride away stood the extraordinary arena at Thysdrus, now El Jem. Seating 35,000, the Thysdrus arena was bested only by the Colosseum. The games were a big part of the culture of this North African province, a way for Rome, with its military ethos, to prove its martial might in brutally theatrical form. So in the Maison de Vénus in Mactar, a mosaic Venus from the first half of the third century AD elegantly adjusts her sandal while roses are scattered on the ground. The iconography all around the goddess relates to the high-octane, often sadistic games that played out in the amphitheatre. In a similar scheme from the neighbouring Tunisian settlement of Thuburbo Maius, Venus is drawn in a chariot, the kind that raced around the Roman circus or amphitheatre or charged across parade grounds.

The North African writer Apuleius – best known for his erotic novella *The Golden Ass* – describes shows preceding the animal or human slaughter of the games, which dramatised popular Greek myths, frequently the story of the Judgement of Paris. Apuleius records that the on-stage Venus who came to 'judge' Paris was naked, beautiful: 'After these another girl made her entrance . . . representing Venus, as Venus looked when she was a virgin. She displayed a perfect figure, her body naked and uncovered except for a piece of sheer silk with which she veiled her comely charms.'*

Across the centuries, Venus – both as an idea and in the form of one of those countless, voiceless 'other girls' paraded for entertainment – seduced both on stage and behind closed doors.

※

Once she had been a champion of real women, but as the divine gloss of the goddess dulled, she was styled a mere woman.

---

* *Metamorphoses*, 10.31, trans. Hanson

Artists such as Rubens regularly used their wives, or their whores, to model as Venus or in Venus-like poses. Cardinal-Infante Ferdinand of Austria, the brother of King Philip IV of Spain, wrote of one of Rubens's paintings in his brother's possession, again depicting the Judgement of Paris: 'The Venus that one finds in the middle of the group is a portrait strongly resembling [Rubens's] own wife, who is without a doubt the prettiest woman here.'

Venus in marble and paint form had become an erotic mixture of the desirable and the unattainable. Come the eighteenth and nineteenth centuries, the Aphrodite-Venuses whom we meet on canvas were regularly the low-class, working girls who ended up as artists' models. Prostitutes themselves came, increasingly, to be nicknamed 'Venuses'. The goddess was now almost exclusively venal, and often venereal.

But in a few, rather eccentric quarters she was still worshipped. Secreted off the respectable country

Peter Paul Rubens, *The Judgement of Paris*, 1637/8.
Oil on panel, Museo del Prado, Madrid

lanes of Buckinghamshire in England is West Wycombe Park, where the lusts of Aphrodite were honoured and adored. This was the stately home of Sir Francis Dashwood, who had fallen in love with the world of antiquity on the Grand Tour, the gap year with attitude enjoyed by many young English nobles. But while many came back simply with artefacts and ideas, Dashwood seems to have returned a convert. He became a priest of Aphrodite. In his extraordinary stately home – still the Dashwood family seat – there are paintings showing Sir Francis and friends as monks, worshipping at the shrine of the goddess. Her image is everywhere, on walls, ceilings, window ledges. In the gardens there is even a temple to her. An entrance underneath the columns – the opening being in the shape of a woman's sex – was said to have witnessed orgiastic rituals in both senses of the word: mysterious and sexual.

But whereas the men enjoying this modern-day Venus-love and the 'gifts of Aphrodite' were of high rank – MPs, bishops, writers, scholars, aristocrats –

the girls in the room were low-class call girls and prostitutes. Aphrodite-Venus had become an agent not of elevation, but of exploitation.

A hugely popular theme for artists and storytellers in the Victorian era was that of the ancient artist Pygmalion and his malleable creation, Galatea. The tale, originally told by Ovid, went that Pygmalion, from Cyprus, was a misogynist. So he fashioned the perfect wife from stone, beautiful, flawless, voiceless. One day he went to make sacrifice at a festival to Aphrodite and prayed that the goddess would give him a spouse like his marble girl. Aphrodite listened kindly, and breathed life into Pygmalion's creation. This offered a perfect trope for the Victorian modus – the notion that women were moulded and made by men.

And in the aftermath of colonial expeditions to the African continent, native-born women were frequently, and lasciviously, described as 'black Venuses'. The remarkable, highly organised Dahomey warrior women from red-earthed Abomey in what is modern-day Benin were styled 'votaries of Venus'. Sara Baartman, the so-called Hottentot Venus, was paraded through Europe's capitals so that a paying public could remark on her pronounced buttocks and genitals. And in cartoons in *Punch* magazine, African women were, for example, portrayed as 'indevirginate . . . eyes being black and burning, like her own fierce skies'. All dreadful cases that tell of subliminal British anxiety about the territories they had annexed. Venus was a thinly-veiled excuse for disturbing and degenerate sexism and racism.

And so the once-feisty goddess had become a functionary. There to excite the male gaze, to nourish an orientalist dominion, simply to decorate fans, fob-watches and glove-trays. No longer a symbol of female empowerment, but of oppression and suppression.

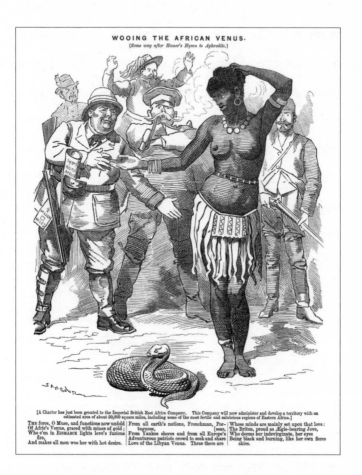

'Adventurous patriots crowd to seek and share Love of the Libyan Venus', *Punch* magazine, 1888

12

A Very Modern Goddess

'My vulva, the horn,
The Boat of Heaven,
Is full of eagerness like the young moon.
My untilled land lies fallow.

As for me, Inanna,
Who will plow my vulva?
Who will plough my high field?
Who will plough my wet ground?'

Dumuzi replied: 'Great Lady, the king will
plough your vulva.
I, Dumuzi, the King, will plough your vulva.'

Inanna: 'Then plough my vulva, man of my heart!
Plough my vulva!' *

---

* 'The Courtship of Inanna and Dumuzi', *c.*2500 BC, trans.
Wolkstein and Kramer

189

So, Aphrodite-Venus, the creature whose naked body pulsed with such power it was terrible to see, had become, ironically, the most-viewed naked female in the Western world. Viewers were sanctioned to become voyeurs.

On 10 March 1914, at 10 a.m., a woman walked into the National Gallery in London. A meat cleaver was hidden in her clothing. She climbed the marble stairs and, after wandering the rooms for ninety minutes, waiting for a lapse in security, made her way directly to one of the most popular paintings in the gallery: *The Toilet of Venus*, known affectionately as 'The Rokeby Venus'. The British public had recently raised £45,000 to keep this painting by Velázquez for the nation when it was sold by its original owner, John Morritt, an MP and landowner who referred to it as his 'fine picture of Venus's backside'.

Taking out her weapon, Mary Richardson, a suffragette, slashed furiously at the canvas – if you look closely today you can still see the fine ridges where the damage has been restored. This was an attack that made headlines across the world. Richardson's fury, she later explained, was because: 'I couldn't stand the way men gawped at it all day long'. As it was reported in *The Times* the following day, Richardson wanted to 'destroy the picture of the most beautiful woman in mythological history!'.

Although the leader of the suffragettes, Emmeline Pankhurst, was styled by some a warrior-goddess, the vandalism of 'The Rokeby Venus' was in protest at Pankhurst's arrest. Aphrodite-Venus had become an attractive packaging for prejudice, nothing more than decorative and demure. No coincidence, surely, that in the nineteenth century another mutilated Venus – the *Venus de Milo* – came to represent the ideal woman of Western civilisation.

While the Cycladic island of Milos was still under Ottoman control, in 1820 a poor farmer discovered, under thick scrub, what would become a modern icon: a marble goddess, originally attributed to Praxiteles, but (as suggested by intriguing evidence on a now-mislaid plinth) was probably sculpted by the journeyman sculptor Alexandros of Antioch in about 80 BC. The foundling was immediately claimed to be Venus. Rescued, traded and then displayed in the Louvre, this sculpture, which had been poorly treated in antiquity – arms broken and then used as infill in a Roman wall – was cherished with extraordinary care and chivalry. When the Louvre was attacked during the Paris Commune the damaged Venus was hidden under the Préfecture of the police. During World War Two she was smuggled out of Paris in the back of a scenery truck from the Comédie-Française and was secreted away in the splendid Château de Valençay in central France.

This is the most replicated of all Aphrodite-Venuses around the globe. And yet the goddess is not the ferocious, charmed result of a cosmic amputation, she is an amputee. Judging by the standards of the day, she is not all-powerful; she is weak, in need of rescue. Venus is no longer creating civilisation, not even just being contained by it: civilisation is revelling in her castration – the armless Venus feeds a ruin-lust. Venus had become primarily an attractive body on to which mankind could project abstract ideas, as was perfectly exemplified by Salvador Dalí's 1936 work, *Venus de Milo with Drawers*. This was a statement artwork inspired not by mighty Aphrodite's story (Dalí opined, 'Nothing is more appropriate to a perfect beauty than a stupid expression. The *Venus de Milo* is the most obvious example of this.'), but by the ideas of Professor Sigmund Freud.

As a young man Freud was a passionate

Venus emerges from the pumice during excavations
in Pompeii in the fifties under the watchful eye of the
Director of Excavations, Amedeo Mauiri

classicist. Having left behind the poor little town of Freiberg in what was then Moravia in 1859, where his father's wool business had collapsed, and which still feels as though it struggles today, his family arrived in the stimulating city of Vienna. Photos here show a straight-backed, seven-year-old Freud, outsize history book on his lap, reading tales of Hannibal and Alexander the Great, and the Greek myths. Aphrodite's legendary birth as a result of castration fascinated Freud and his life's work came to be to explore what, as individuals and as a civilisation, we choose to do with desire.

From the cold little kitchen in Vienna ideas started to pour: the notion of the unconscious as a reservoir of impulses; treating the mind like an archaeological dig; uncovering memories; recognising that the past is present in our daily lives. Psycho-sexuality and its psycho-dynamics became a central doctrine in Freud's early work and the value of Eros' lover Psyche was amplified – Freud invented the term psycho-analysis in honour of the psyche – a Greek concept meaning the soul, spirit, life-breath, the inner mind and Eros' consort. But Aphrodite-Venus has been side-lined; for Freud it was really all about her trouble-making boy, Eros.

Having been expelled from Nazi-occupied Austria by the Gestapo when he was eighty-two, Freud settled in genteel Hampstead, north London. His study there is crammed with artefacts from the ancient world – a plethora of Venuses and Aphrodites and Astartes among them. On his desk sits one modelled on the *Knidian Aphrodite*. Another Venus favourite, portrayed with a mirror, represented to him the narcissism of the female, making up for her lack of phallus by staring at her own lovely face. Like Caesar, Freud wore a ring emblazoned with Greek goddesses, and Princess Marie Bonaparte, one of his clients, gave him a bronze figurine of Aphrodite as a thank-you gift. But it is Eros who dominates the room. Because in his pioneering, flawed research, the psychoanalyst distorted and amplified an ideological duality which existed in part in the ancient world, but which did not stem from the long-learnt lessons of the goddess's life story.

An idle reflection, tentatively set down in the early 1920s and then codified, became foundational to Freudian thought. Freud's notion was this: that Eros, representing stimulation, activation, ambition, lust for life, desire, was in constant struggle with the human death drive. And that the conflict and collaboration between Eros and absence, Death, explained the complexity of the life experience. For Freud, civilisation served Eros, not vice versa. In *Civilization and its Discontents* (1930) he wrote: 'And now, I think, the meaning of the evolution of civilisation is no longer obscure to us. It must present the struggle between Eros and Death, between the instinct of life and the instinct of destruction as it works itself out in the human species.'

Freud's ideas were prodigiously influential.

Whereas Aphrodite, and her prehistoric ancestors, had combined both negative and positive impulses in one body, Freud presented these as warring poles. His identification of the power of what he called 'the pleasure principle' and 'wish-fulfilment' established psychoanalytical guidelines that were eagerly employed by the advertising industry as triggers to tap into an individual's inner yearnings and desires. So we have Gillette's Venus razors for women, promising to 'Reveal the goddess in you'. Dove soap for soft skin, and Venus-branded pomegranate juice. The gifts of Aphrodite were used now not to bind communities, but to aid self-fulfilment and self-absorption.

But there were others who used the Venus brand in other ways. The ancient astrological sign for Venus is familiar to all of us, even if we don't realise it. Either representing Aphrodite's hand mirror, or her necklace, or a woman's sex, it has appeared in medical journals and on latrines for decades to symbolise

Women's liberation demonstration in New York, 1970s.
Venus' astrological sign has been adapted
and is emblazoned on banners

the female. Appropriately, ♀ is also the symbol for Aphrodite-Kypris' metal, copper. (Incidentally, it is Venus' lover Mars' astrological sign ♂ – a shield and erect spear – that has been used as the symbol of the male.) Christians added a crossbar to make the pagan Venus symbol more crucifix-like, and in the 1970s a fist was drawn into the circle to signify not just the female, but female resistance.

And while the inevitable appearance of the goddess of love in modern-day pop songs can be banal, some performers have played with her adamite appeal (popular romantic music, we should remember, owes much to the medieval songs of the troubadours). Bananarama – covering Shocking Blue's Transatlantic 1969 hit 'Venus' – imagined the goddess as a bubble-gum pink parody in a sea-shell and a gyrating she-devil, and opined in their own 1986 international chart-buster, that: 'her weapons were her crystal eyes'. Kylie Minogue's eleventh studio album was called *Aphrodite*, and Lady Gaga referenced 'Aphrodite lady, sea-shell bikini' and prayed to one of her Erotes, Himeros – a representation of unrequited love. When Beyoncé launched a series of goddess-inspired photographs, pregnant with twins, she presented herself to the world as a golden spirit of the sea and of fertility drawing from potent African, European and Asian role models – Venus included.

Aphrodite-Venus has enjoyed a long journey from the fire-blazing, Middle Eastern deity to a glamour-girl, used in the twenty-first century to sell everything from cocktails to sex toys. Every 14 February, 200 million red roses are grown for the global Valentine's Day market – Aphrodite's flower is still exchanged as a token of love. As an idea and an image, Aphrodite-Venus is present in our lives, in both Western and Eastern cultures. The goddess is at once elemental and a transitory cultural meme. We remember her when we talk of aphrodisiacs, eroticism, cupidity, cosmetics, being Paphian and, hopefully infrequently, of venereal disease. Latterly,

her image is once again being used to promote the
idea that female sexuality has potency and potential
– as it first was in prehistory. She appears, still, to be
immortal.

Women and men have petitioned the goddess for
millennia:

> *Cypris ...*
>
> *now grant a great favour*
> *In turn for this little one, as is your wont,*
> *She only asks for her and her husband*
> *To be of one mind, heart and soul.*[*]

Until love is redundant, the goddess of love looks
unlikely to lose her appeal.

---

[*] *The Greek Anthology*, 6.209, trans. Chloe Tye

Conclusion

Conclusion

Muse, tell me the deeds of Golden Aphrodite the Cyprian, who stirs up sweet passion in the gods and subdues the tribes of mortal men and birds that fly in the air and all the many creatures that the dry land rears and all the sea. *

... you alone are the guiding power of the universe and without you nothing emerges into the shining sunlit world to grow in joy and loveliness ... †

---

* *Homeric Hymn* 5.1–6, trans. Evelyn-White
† Lucretius, *On the Nature of the Universe*, 1.21–3, trans. Latham

Of all the ancient goddesses, why is Venus so obdurate? When Aphrodite holds up her famous mirror, what reflection is delivered back? Is it simply the enduring popularity of what she represents – a delight in beauty, a fear of and fascination for female and queer sexuality and the long and dangerous relationship between sex and violence?

Is she an early conduit for our petty delight in another's misfortune, another's misdemeanours? The clickbait of a pre-Twitter age? The myth of Aphrodite and Ares or Venus and Mars being discovered by Hephaestus or Vulcan fed a salacious, net-curtain-twitching interest in adultery, and in women in

Joachim Wtewael, *Mars and Venus Discovered
by the Gods*, *c.*1603/4. Oil on copper, currently in
a private collection

particular being caught in a compromising position, from antiquity until the turn of the new millennium. Now real-life stories of infidelity, slut-shaming and revenge porn saturate the digital conversation.

This goddess is a candescent creature – and all that bright light will bring shade.

USAAF B-24J Armed Venus, which flew with the 494th Bombardment Group in the Second World War, and was retired from service in July 1945

Yet Aphrodite can be a catalyst not just for our baser moments, but for our most elevated. She is a vehicle not just for passion, but for philosophy. A sounding-board we can use to think with as well as to feel. As the female philosopher Diotima argues in Plato's *Symposium*, it is Aphrodite's influence that pushes Eros on the path to seek beauty. Desire is a quest for the beautiful – whatever 'the beautiful' might mean. Desire is the thing that makes us feel great about the world and therefore be great in it. It is the life force that spurs us on to do, to be, to think. The point of love is not gratification but symbiosis; the point of human-heartedness to nourish wisdom and the swelling joy of human relations – physical, intellectual, social, civilisational. In the *Symposium*, Eros becomes man's partner and 'universal guide'. Recent scholarship has supported the notion that Diotima might in fact be a cover name for Pericles' fabulously smart courtesan-consort Aspasia. It could be that all these ideas around the nature of eroticism and platonic love, the gifts of Aphrodite, are not just grandstanding sophistries from privileged men but genuine conversations between men and women, and include a female point of view.

There's one quiet place where the 'mixing-up' goddess can still be found. On Cyprus, Aphrodite's Isle, once a year, on Good Friday, women and children decorate a bier with flowers. Mothers and grandmothers chat in small, Greek-speaking villages as they pick and weave the garlands together. They are tending a representation of the body of Christ, but the tradition goes way back to the pre-Christian world. In antiquity, every year the women of the community here would make an image of Aphrodite's dead lover, Adonis, and lay it on a wooden plank decorated with flowers. Processing around the corpse of this young man, prematurely cut down, they would slash and beat their breasts, mimicking Aphrodite's reaction to the death of her beloved. They remembered that Aphrodite was so enraptured with her lover that she effected his resurrection; maybe their efforts could achieve the same results. Using the flowers she has sponsored for millennia, sharing the wine the goddess has always approved, these women remember that the pain of love can be ameliorated by the balm of unity, of compassion and companionship.

Aphrodite's children by Ares are indeed Deimos and Phobos, Dread and Fear, but also Harmony. And perhaps what Aphrodite asks us to do when we commemorate her is not to seek the desire that destroys, but that unites, that pulls communities together, not apart. She is both the wound and the bandage. The ancients understood that desire is worthy of respect. Human relations of all kinds are hard. The life story of Aphrodite from prehistory to the present, invented by human minds, can help us to decode human desire a little: to make it our ally, not our undoing.

Perhaps, then, it is best to think of her as the

Conclusion

Greeks did – the goddess who mixes things up. Not a deity of raw, unilateral, single-minded ambition or passion but a consequential force, a reminder of what happens when we impose those passions on others and on the world around us. Aphrodite-Venus, the heavenly, Paphian queen, is far more than just a gorgeous goddess of love: she is an incarnation of, and a guide through, the messy, troubling, quixotic, quickening business of mortal life.

> *Do you not see what a great goddess Aphrodite*
> *is? She whom you can neither name nor measure,*
> *how great she is by nature from how great a*
> *thing she comes through. She nourishes you and*
> *me and all the mortals. And as proof, so that you*
> *might not only comprehend this in words, I will*
> *show you by deed, the strength of the goddess.*
> *On the one hand, earth desires rain when the dry*
> *barren ground is in need of moisture on account*
> *of drought and on the other hand the revered sky*

when it is filled with rain by Aphrodite desires

that it fall on the earth; and when the two mingle

into the same thing, they beget everything for

us and at the same time they nurture everything

through which the mortal race lives and grows. *

---

* Euripides, Fragment 898ᴋ, from an unidentified play, trans. Collard

Acknowledgements

✳

Across the years, many people have helped me in my quest for Aphrodite. My debt to those scholars and archaeologists who have broken ground before me is legion. Heartfelt thanks, in the first instance, are due to Dr Andreas Pittas. Andreas recognised my decades-long passion for the goddess and gently and persistently persuaded me to continue to follow in her path. Ömer Koç offered odysseys and reminded me of the timeless tumult and brilliant balm of the sea. Of course, enormous credit is due to Alan Samson and Julian Alexander. Patient, stimulating, always full of wit and wisdom – they are empathetic word-merchants and ever-inspiring pleasure-seekers. The Leventis family and

Titina Loizides have been hugely supportive on journeys from London to Aphrodite's Isle. Holly Harley, Linden Lawson, Hannah Cox and Jo Whitford have perfectly piloted the Aphrodite-barque home to port. Gül Pulhan and dear, departed Jacqueline Karageorghis and Angelos Delivorias have all offered advice, knowledge and sagacity. As has dearest Paul Cartledge – who has once again surpassed himself. Thank you Paul. Tim Whitmarsh and Bert Smith were Hermes-like in the speed and acuity of their responses to Aphroditic queries. In 2007 Professor Peltenberg guided me through Aphrodite's pre-history, he is a great loss. Many academic colleagues answered my late-night pleas for help – I thank just some here: Juliet Claxton, Kate Cooper, Irving Finkel, Thomas Kiely, Peter Fischer, Dany Nobus, Armand D'Angour, Paul Roberts, Antony Makrinos, Barbara Graziosi. May stood shivering in very little on Paphos beach, Sorrel read out tracks from late antiquity until late in the night, Philip Sellars, Mary Cranitch, Shula Subramaniam, Ruth Sessions, Nigel Gardner, Jack McInnes and Alan Hill all aided in broadcasting Aphrodite-Venus – helping to share years of research with a wider world. Tim Knight stood with me on a freezing December shore, with snow in the air, to capture the strange columns of water in the south-west of the island of Cyprus that rise up when the winter tides hit the coast at 90 degrees – three or four metres high, a seawater shaft that maybe witnesses the perceived birth of Aphrodite herself. My darling mother and late father, exemplars of unconditional love, first nourished a fascination for the lives of others. Jane, as ever, put this, and all of us, before herself. She is love incarnate. Adrian Evans has now endured close on three decades of my scholarly and emotional obsessions, thank you for your unerring good humour, inspiration and abidance throughout.

I marked up the first proofs for this book in one hospital in London and the final proofs in another. Thank you to all the NHS staff and carers worldwide who care for our loved ones, and also care for those who sit and wait, because they love.

Illustrations

Illustrations

PLATE SECTION

Illustrations

Select Bibliography

* Bailey, A. (2011), *Velázquez and The Surrender of Breda: The Making of a Masterpiece*. New York: Henry Holt and Company.

* Beard, M. (2008), *Pompeii: The Life of a Roman Town*. London: Profile Books.

* Boatswain, T. (2005), *A Traveller's History of Cyprus*. Gloucestershire: Chastleton Travel/Arris Publishing Ltd.

* Breitenberger, B. (2007), *Aphrodite and Eros: The Development of Erotic Mythology in Early Greek Poetry and Cult*. New York: Routledge.

* Bull, M. (2006), *The Mirror of the Gods: Classical Mythology in Ancient Art*. London: Penguin Books.

Select Bibliography

✴ Burke, J. (2018), *The Italian Renaissance Nude*.
London and New Haven: Yale University Press.

✴ Campbell, D.A. (ed. and trans.) (2015), *Greek Lyric,
Volume III: Stesichorus, Ibycus, Simonides, and Others*.
Loeb Classical Library 476. London: W. Heinemann.

✴ Carson, A. (2003), *If Not, Winter: Fragments of
Sappho*. London: Virago Press.

✴ Collard, C. and Cropp., M. (eds and trans.) (2014),
Euripides: Fragments. Loeb Classical Library 506.
Cambridge, MA: Harvard University Press.

✴ D-scholia in C. G. Heyne, ed., *Homeri Ilias* (Oxford,
1834).

✴ Dalby, A. (2005), *The Story of Venus*. London: The
British Museum Press.

✴ Dalí. S. (2013), trans. H.M. Chevalier, *The Secret Life
of Salvador Dalí*. New York: Dover Publications, Inc.

✴ D'Angour, A. (2019), *Socrates in Love: The Making of
a Philosopher*. London: Bloomsbury Publishing.

* Delcourt, M., trans. J. Nicholson (1961), *Hermaphrodite: Myths and Rites of the Bisexual Figure in Classical Antiquity*. London: Studio Books/Longacre Press Ltd.

* De Shong Meador, B. (2000), *Inanna, Lady of Largest Heart: Poems of the Sumerian High Priestess Enheduanna*. Austin, TX: University of Texas Press.

* Empereur, J.-Y. (2000), *A Short Guide to the Græco-Roman Museum, Alexandria*. Alexandria: Harpocrates Publishing.

* Evans, M. and Weppelmann, S. (eds) (2016), *Botticelli Reimagined*. London: V&A Publishing.

* Evelyn-White, H.G. (trans.) (1914), *Hesiod: Works and Days*. Accessed online 12/04/19: http://www.sacred-texts.com/cla/hesiod/works.htm

* Evelyn-White H.G. (2008), The Project Gutenberg EBook of *Hesiod, The Homeric Hymns, and Homerica*, by Homer and Hesiod. Accessed online 12/04/2019: https://www.gutenberg.org/files/348/348-h/348-h.htm

Select Bibliography

* Fitton, J. (2002), *Peoples of the Past: Minoans*. London: The British Museum Press.

* Fletcher, J. (2008), *Cleopatra the Great*. London: Hodder & Stoughton Ltd.

* Freud, S. and Riviere, J. (1930), *Civilization and its Discontents*. London: Leonard & Virginia Woolf at the Hogarth Press, and the Institute of Psycho-analysis.

* Gay, P. (1989), *Freud: A Life for Our Time*. London: Papermac/MacMillan Publishers Ltd.

* Goddio, F. and Masson-Berghoff, A. (eds) (2016), *Sunken Cities*. London: Thames & Hudson Ltd, in collaboration with the British Museum.

* Godwin, J. (2000), *The Pagan Dream of the Renaissance*. Grand Rapids, MI: Phanes Press, Inc.

* Goodison, L. and Morris, C. (eds) (1998), *Ancient Goddesses: The Myths and The Evidence*. London: The British Museum Press.

* Graziosi, B. (2013), *The Gods of Olympus: A History*. London: Profile Books.

✳ Grigson, G. (1976), *The Goddess of Love: The Birth, Triumph, Death and Return of Aphrodite*. London: Constable & Co.

✳ Hadjigavriel, L., Hatzaki, M. and Theodotou Anagnostopoulou, D. (eds) (2018), *The Venus Paradox*. Nicosia: A.G. Leventis Gallery.

✳ Hall, E. and Wyles, R. (eds) (2008), *New Directions in Ancient Pantomime*. Oxford: Oxford University Press.

✳ Hanson, J. A. (ed. and trans.) (1989), *Apuleius: Metamorphoses*. Cambridge, MA: Harvard University Press.

✳ Henderson, J. (ed. and trans.) (2007), *Aristophanes V: Fragments*. Cambridge, MA: Harvard University Press.

✳ Hunter, R. L. and Hunter, R. (2004) *Plato's Symposium*. Oxford: Oxford University Press.

✳ Jacob, C. and De Polignac, F. (eds) (2000), *Alexandria, Third Century BC: The Knowledge of the World in a Single City*. Alexandria: Harpocrates Publishing.

* Jenkins, I., with Farge, C. and Turner, V. (2015), *Defining Beauty: The Body in Ancient Greek Art.* London: The British Museum Press.

* Jones, W.H.S. (trans.) (1918), *Pausanias. Description of Greece, Volume I: Books 1–2 (Attica and Corinth).* Loeb Classical Library 93. Cambridge, MA: Harvard University Press.

* Karageorghis, J. (2005), *Kypris: The Aphrodite of Cyprus: Ancient Sources and Archaelogical Evidence.* Nicosia: A.G. Leventis Foundation.

* Latham, R.E. (trans.) (1994), *Lucretius: On the Nature of the Universe.* London: Penguin Books.

* Lloyd-Jones, H. (ed. and trans.) (2014), *Sophocles: Fragments.* Loeb Classical Library 483. Cambridge, MA: Harvard University Press.

* Lombardo, S. (trans.) (2000), *Homer: Odyssey.* Indianapolis: Hackett Publishing Company.

* — (2005), *Aeneid: Virgil.* Indianapolis: Hackett Publishing Company.

* MacLeod, R. (ed.) (2001), *The Library of Alexandria: Centre of Learning in the Ancient World*. New York/ London: I.B. Tauris & Co. Ltd.

* Mair, A.W. (trans.) (1928), *Oppian. Colluthus. Tryphiodorus*. Loeb Classical Library 219. London: William Heinemann.

* Mitchell Havelock, C. (2010), *The Aphrodite of Knidos and Her Successors: A Historical Review of the Female Nude in Greek Art*. Ann Arbor, MI: University of Michigan Press.

* Nixey, C. (2017), *The Darkening Age*. London: Macmillan.

* Paton. W.R. (trans.), Tueller, M.A (rev.) (2014), *The Greek Anthology, Volume 1: Book 1: Christian Epigrams. Book 2: Christodorus of Thebes in Egypt. Book 3: The Cyzicene Epigrams. Book 4: The Proems of the Different Anthologies. Book 5: The Amatory Epigrams. Book 6: The Dedicatory Epigrams*. Cambridge, MA: Harvard University Press.

* Pekin A. K. and Kangal, S. (eds) (2007), *Istanbul: 8000 Years Brought to Daylight: Marmaray, Metro, Sultanahmet Excavations*. Istanbul: Vehbi Koç Foundation.

* Rackham, H. (trans.) (1933), *Cicero: De Natura Deorum*. Loeb Classical Library. Cambridge, MA: Harvard University Press.

* Rayor, D. (2016), 'Reimagining the Fragments of Sappho through Translation'. In *Reimagining the Fragments of Sappho through Translation*. Leiden, The Netherlands: Brill.

* Roberts, P. (2013), *Life and Death in Pompeii and Herculaneum*. London: The British Museum Press.

* Rowlandson, J. (ed.) (1998), *Women and Society in Greek and Roman Egypt: A Sourcebook*. Cambridge: Cambridge University Press.

* Selover, S.L. (2015), 'Excavating War: The Archaeology of Conflict in Early Chalcolithic to Early Bronze III Central and South-eastern Anatolia'. PhD thesis, University of Chicago, Illinois.

* Severis, D.C. (2001), *Cypriot Art: From the Costakis and Leto Severis Collection*. Cambridge: The Fitzwilliam Museum.

* Shabti, A. (trans.) (1978), Ibykos' works in The Israel Museum Catalogue *Aphrodite* No. 184, Jerusalem: Central Press.

* Shakespeare, W., ed. M. Hattaway (2009), *As You Like It. The New Cambridge Shakespeare*. Cambridge: Cambridge University Press.

* — (1998) *A Midsummer Night's Dream*. New York: Signet Classic.

* — Spencer, T.J.B. (ed.) (1967), *Romeo and Juliet. The New Penguin Shakespeare*. London: Penguin.

* Showerman, G. (trans.) (1914), *Ovid: Heroides. Amores*. Revised by G. P. Goold. Loeb Classical Library. Cambridge, MA: Harvard University Press.

* Skinner, M.B. (2005), *Sexuality in Greek and Roman Culture*. Malden, MA/London/Victoria: Blackwell Publishing Ltd.

❋ Smith, A.C. and Pickup, S. (eds) (2010), *Brill's Companion to Aphrodite*. Leiden: Brill.

❋ Stampolides, N.C. and Parlama, L. (eds) (2000), *Athens: The City Beneath the City: Antiquities from the Metropolitan Railway Excavations*. Athens: Kapon Editions, with the Greek Ministry of Culture, N.P. Goulandris Foundation and the Museum of Cycladic Art.

❋ Sugimoto, D.T. (ed.) (2014), *Transformation of a Goddess: Ishtar – Astarte – Aphrodite*: (Orbis Biblicus Et Orientalis). Germany: Academic Press, Fribourg Vandenhoeck & Ruprecht, Göttingen.

❋ Taylor, T. (1792), *The Hymns of Orpheus*. Accessed online 11/04/2019: https://www.sacred-texts.com/cla/hoo/index.htm

❋ Thornton, B.S. (1997), *Eros: The Myth of Ancient Greek Sexuality*. Boulder, CO: Westview Press.

❋ Usener, H. (1907), *Der Heilige Tychon*. Leipzig: Teubner.

❋ Vellacott, P. (1953), *Euripides: Alcestis and Other Plays*. London: Penguin Group.

* von Sacher-Masoch, L., trans. F. Savage (2018), *Venus in Furs* (illustrated). Clap Publishing.

* Vout, C. (2018), *Classical Art: A Life History from Antiquity to the Present*. Princeton and Oxford: Princeton University Press.

* Ward, J. and Frances Jones, E. (eds), trans E.G. Schreiber and T.E. Maresca (1977), *The Commentary on the First Six Books of the Aeneid of Vergil Commonly Attributed to Bernardus Silvestris*. Lincoln, NE: University of Nebraska Press.

* West, M.L. (trans.) (1993), *Greek Lyric Poetry*. Oxford: Oxford University Press.

* Wilkinson. P. (2017), *Pompeii: An Archaeological Guide*. New York/London: I.B. Tauris & Co. Ltd.

* Wolkstein, D. and Kramer, S.N. (1983), *Inanna, Queen of Heaven and Earth: Her Stories and Hymns from Sumer*. New York: Harper & Row.

Index

Index

Index

Index